To Live and Die With Dignity

A Guide To Living Wills

by

D1059756

Samuel L. Peluso, Esq.

Edited by Mary Lou Diecker

Edited by Mary Lou Diecker
Cover design by Thomas Taylor, of Thomcatt Graphics

VISTA PUBLISHING, INC.
473 Broadway
Long Branch, NJ 07740
(908) 229-4545

This publication is designed to provide accurate and authoritative information in regard to the subject matter covered. It is sold with the understanding that if legal advice or other expert assistance is required, the services of a competent professional should be sought.

Printed and bound in the United States of America on acid-free stock

ISBN: 1-880254-01-8
Library of Congress Catalog Card Number: 91-75021

U.S.A. Price $19.95
Canada Price $26.95

DEDICATION

To all those people who are afraid of their future,
may they find comfort from whence comfort comes.

ACKNOWLEDGMENTS

I would like to thank all those who assisted in this endeavor. With regard to technical content and reference material, special thanks to my legal clerk David Foley, and to Helen Peluso and Marlene Johnsen.

A dynamic, knowledgeable and dedicated group known as Professional Healthcare Associates, Inc., was an absolute pleasure to work with.

To my publisher and editor, I am indebted for their constant encouragement, confidence and motivation. Both are highly professional and immensely capable.

Most of all, I thank my wife Jody, daughter Lena, my parents and the powers that be, as I believe they have a hand in everything I do.

CONTENTS

Preface

PREFACE

What is a Living Will? It is simply a document which specifies, in advance, the nature and duration of medical care one would prefer under a given set of circumstances.

Why in advance? By its very nature, medical care is often required when its recipient is functioning at less than 100% capacity. Perhaps the problem necessitating medical treatment is one involving loss of mental capacity or consciousness. If this were to happen, how would your wishes be known to doctors or family had you not stated them earlier?

As technology stretches the boundaries of knowledge, it is also pushing the limits of life itself, often beyond that which nature may tolerate. Although knowledge is being acquired at an ever-increasing rate, our bodies and minds remain either at a God-given constant or plod toward perfection through the process of evolution. The ever-broadening gap that results may be bridged by a Living Will.

Many readers may have been exposed to the realities of a grave decline in another's physical or mental condition. Many have also witnessed the driving resistance of medical technology to that deterioration. This conflict is frequently encountered during the care-giving and dying processes of friends or relatives. The recognition of this conflict often leads a survivor to consider having a Living Will.

The need for a Living Will did not arise in a vacuum. Our forefathers were not subjected to the many encroachments upon their lives that we experience. They had no highways, supermarkets or residential complexes crowding them from each and every direction. They were not required to seek out and structure their privacy, as it was simply a part of life. This is not so, however, for the present-day American.

We are forced to struggle and clamor for privacy. With neighbors pressing from each direction and with government in our hip pocket, there is little opportunity to escape and enjoy the serenity of a private moment. Unfortunately, this loss of privacy continues through the final days of our lives. Gone is the time when Grandma stopped being quite herself, was cared for by her family, and died quietly one night in the bed in which she was born.

Today there are bright lights, unfamiliar medical staffers, feeding tubes, respirators and catheters. Nursing homes, radical surgery and drug therapy often extend life. The intrusiveness of and complete surrender to these processes, however, can have dubious effects on its quality. This may also result in a dehumanized, painful, and isolated end to our lives.

There is obviously great value in medical technology. It is as likely a gift from God as birth itself for so long as it similarly gives, sustains, and perpetuates life. When medical technology becomes parasitic, however, and does little more than pathetically reign over the process of dying, causing physical and psychological pain, it becomes nothing more than a cancer that should be eradicated from the patient host. In fact, in certain circumstances, it has been said that treatment which is supposed to prolong life may be little more than the inducement of physiological activity in a corpse. [1]

These concepts have often been referred to as "dying with dignity." This is a misnomer, in part, for it is "life with dignity" which we seek. Dignity in life and death may be planned for in a Living Will.

The phrases "dignity in life" or "dignity in death " impart a sense of righteousness and faithfulness to our essence. But what is our essence? We are autonomous yet socially dependent creatures. We need warmth and security as well as freedom. We can be maintained with a meager sustenance, but can only flourish when nurtured in an environment of affection and caring. Hence, your Living Will should establish guidelines that will permit auton-

3

omy and self-determination while not excluding the benefits medical advances have to offer. You may wish to choose a comforting environment for healthcare that will provide a desirable level of warmth and personal contact. Then the fear of having our dying process hopelessly, helplessly and painfully extended may be confronted and set aside.

If "dignity in life" or "dignity in death" mean something different to you, then so should your Living Will differ from mine. The documents should be similar only insofar as their purpose, which is to direct and control medical treatment in the event that, at some time in the future, our physical or mental condition does not permit us the opportunity to do so.

This book contains sufficient health, medical, and legal information to assist you in making informed and intelligent decisions concerning future healthcare and to memorialize those choices in a Living Will. TO LIVE AND DIE WITH DIGNITY is not a substitute for legal or medical advice from professionals with whom you may share unique concerns or circumstances. In fact, it is my specific recommendation that you confer with such professionals regarding this and any related topic.

CHAPTER 1

WHY A LIVING WILL

It is a natural and common occurrence to avoid thinking or talking about and planning for the eventualities of sickness, injury, or death. We frequently and quite naturally develop an "it won't happen to me" mentality.

It is also likely that for many of us, traumatic, painful or chronic illness will not occur during our youth. Some may even grow old and die without having experienced any debilitating disease or condition. It is a fact of life, however, that we all may suffer illness or injury that requires care, perhaps of an extraordinary or life-sustaining nature.

With any such medical condition or crisis, we find ourselves viewing life and death from a new perspective. These ultimate realities must then be dealt with "hands on" and no longer deferred by a false sense of invulnerability, a fantasy born of fear or ignorance. The dramatic and unforgiving nature of certain illnesses snaps us into a hyper-reality. For example, we can walk, talk, be independent and productive for what was to that point a lifetime. Then, a moment of trauma or interrupted oxygen flow to the brain could drastically change our world and that of those around us forever. In the best of circumstances, some knowledge of the issues surrounding these situations is essential. In the worst of circumstances, the lack of forethought is unforgivable. Any medical crisis, whether it develops as we age or shocks us in our youth, demands that we confront occurrences that are out of the ordinary scope of experience and contemplation.

Common Sense Planning

The first area of planning should be for the eventuality of medical care, as it is so likely to be encountered. As with most decisions, the selection of healthcare alternatives that are planned with careful consideration, unpressured by the stress of the moment, will invariably yield the best results.

We may plan for thirty years to pay off a mortgage early but leave the selection of a healthcare facility or course of treatment to circumstance. We might spend half a lifetime preparing for a job or retirement that may never arrive yet fail to discuss the inevitability of our deaths, which is truly our final endeavor.

My law office has assisted many clients in preparing their Last Will and Testament wherein plans for asset distribution and funeral arrangements are discussed and written. The vast majority of clients, however, must be reminded of their opportunity to plan for their healthcare through a Living Will.

Although it is laudable to plan our estates for the benefit of others, it is a greater act of compassion and self-respect to plan for our personal care. It is easy to give away material items that we will no longer need. It is quite different, however, to lift from our family the burden of making what may be considered a life or death decision. Having a Last Will is sound business and family planning. Having a Living Will is a courageous and honorable act.

Exploring choices for medical care does not need to be difficult. It presents an opportunity to make decisions that may enhance or save one's life. This annoints us with a level of satisfaction, fulfillment and security greater than that which accompanies a prepaid mortgage. It is better to plan for our physiological degeneration, as best we can, than it is to hide our heads in the sand in a futile and irresponsible effort to avoid life.

Many of us pride ourselves on the way we plan, examine our options and make decisions. Where will we go to school and what type of education will we pursue? Will we marry? If we choose to have children, when will we begin those new lives? This is commendable, but the planning should not stop there. It is critical that we examine our entire future and plan ahead for all of its eventualities.

Safeguard Your Choices

What a Living Will can do, most significantly, is reserve for you a treasure trove of self-determination. Those decisions a Living Will may include are of an intimate nature, implemented when you will be the closest to your Maker since birth.

Refuse to permit a hospital protocol, a court or medical provider to take from you this opportunity of a lifetime. Nor should the possibility that you may be incompetent or unable to communicate your intentions steal away this God-given and legal right to live and die upon your own responsible terms, naturally and with dignity.

The concept of dignity in this context goes beyond saving one from existing in a painful or physically morbid condition. In fact, depending upon the individual, it has little or nothing to do with that. Dignity in life and death is how each of us defines it. Changes in behavior such as incontinence, mental confusion or loss of ambulatory functions, though new and unpleasant, should not be confused with indignities of the type and nature to be avoided by the withholding or withdrawal of life-sustaining measures.

A person is never undignified. Rather, he or she may only be treated so. A Living Will is not designed to provide convenience. Dependence of the afflicted upon family and healthcare institutions should never attempt to be avoided through the utilization of a Living Will. A Living Will does not tinker with life's natural rhythms, needs and requirements.

That which many people believe to be dehumanizing or an affront to their dignity often occurs in the latter stages of life and while approaching death. The unwanted use of artificial and mechanical life-sustaining companions such as respirators or feeding tubes are frequently cited culprits. As you will discover in later chapters, the removal or avoidance of these perceived indignities do not happen automatically or with great ease. There may be courts, family, institutional intervention and other impediments to the fulfillment of one's wishes. A thoroughly considered and written plan specifying the type, intensity and duration of life-sustaining treatment is the best insurance we have against unwanted medical and legal intervention.

Is this an issue that may impact you, a friend or a family member? Consider this: Roughly 2.1 million Americans die each year, many of them in hospitals and nursing homes where life-prolonging medical treatment is readily available. 2 Therefore, the likelihood that one may be placed on a regimen including life-sustaining measures is greatly increased.

Those who are closest to this conflict have recognized that the autonomy to make decisions pertaining to life-support programs belongs first to the patient.

> *"The most important key to appropriate ethical management of the initiation and withdrawal of life support is constant awareness of the true source of authority. Although the physicians must often be authoritative about the options available to patients, all involved should recognize that the actual authority over the patient never resides with the physician. Patients alone, or their legal surrogates, have the right to control what happens to them."* 3

It is easy to sit at the kitchen table with family or friends and expound one's opinion regarding medical conditions and treatment in a speculative and non-committal fashion. It is quite a different matter, however, to have placed before you a legal document which, when executed, could hasten your death. There is no doubt that this occasion might be accompanied by an air of solemnity and hesitancy. Although a Living Will is easily revocable, there can be a sense of finality when signing such a document.

Knowledge Builds Confidence

As in most situations, information and knowledge will ease this process by instilling confidence. This in turn strengthens resolve and commitment. Thereafter, hesitancy and vacillation are appropriately set aside and a sense of comfort and peace of mind wells up from within. For example, while attempting to make a decision on this subject, a knowledge of the medical community and certain terms and conditions is necessary.

There should also exist a method of checking the decisions stated in your Living Will so as to be confident their propriety is not lamented. One recommendation is to make the decision for yourself as if it were being made for the person you hold most dear. This will ensure a document where you are treated with the care and respect often reserved for others, but frequently overlooked for one's self.

The place to start our discussion of creating a Living Will is in acknowledging that a medical condition resulting in the need for life-sustaining medical care can happen to anyone. In fact, as will be revealed, this must be considered a probability rather than a possibility. With that in mind, the following chapters will provide an explanation of certain conditions, treatments, medical and legal concepts and terminology. Please note that this information is not intended to cause undue concern or alarm, but rather to familiarize the reader with the requisite vocabulary and tools for creating a Living Will.

It is my experience that those who wish to have a Living Will are not doomsayers, but rather, are upbeat and responsible people with a positive approach to life and all that goes with it, including death. Their wish is to probe the issue, resolve it, set it aside, and continue with their life knowing that an otherwise problematic contingency has been addressed.

Our frailties, although not easily confronted, understood or pleasant, are nonetheless our condition in both good and bad times. This is quite different, however, from another concern for anyone planning his or her future healthcare, that being medical technology. There is great value in technology, but it is foreign to our condition and may be accepted or rejected at will. A Living Will permits you to accept technologically advanced treatment when it is good for you, and to reject it when it is not.

There exist a myriad of medications, treatments, surgical procedures, and life-support apparatus that may be utilized to extend life or the dying process for what may seem an indefinite time. Some of the advancements which are available today did not exist just a few years ago. Virtually all bodily systems, including the heart, kidney and lungs may be sustained or supported by advanced machines and therapies. We may be fed, hydrated and medicated through tubes and have brain activity monitored for signs of life.

Many of today's modern diagnostic machinery has taken the guesswork out of discerning a patient's condition or possibility of recovery. A doctor no longer sits by the bedside unaware if vital bodily functions continue, hoping the patient will "pull through." Many of the bodily operations which are most revealing in terms of one's health or possibility of recovery can be measured easily and with as much accuracy as one's weight. That is why if your Living Will clearly expresses your requests, the likelihood of them being properly administered is excellent.

CHAPTER 2

MEDICAL TERMINOLOGY

Any decision pertaining to your healthcare must be made in a knowing and intelligent manner. This is required under the law and should be expected of ourselves. Although being a competent adult entitles us to execute a Living Will, it does not necessarily qualify each of us to do the job well. It is also necessary to have a basic understanding of certain medical terms and conditions to ensure that what you wish is accurately stated to your lawyer and understood by your doctor. I strongly urge that anyone wishing to have a Living Will speak with and involve a knowledgeable attorney and physician.

To help understand the perplexing world of health-care technology, the following are descriptions of the more common forms of life-sustaining technology and diagnostic procedures presently utilized. Please note that use of one or more of these does not mean that the patient is in a life-threatening state. Such technology may be used in the healing process and is not, by design or purpose, dehumanizing or to be feared. It is only when such methods are used in a manner inconsistent with your wishes that there should be concern.

Cardiac Monitor. A device that permits a continuous reading of heartbeats and measures their rate and rhythm. Also referred to as a monitor or heart monitor.

Cardiopulmonary Resuscitation. CPR is a resuscitative procedure for sudden death or the cessation of heart and lung activity. CPR is a temporary measure which, when started immediately, increases the chance of survival by restarting the heart and providing artificial respiration when breathing stops. The probability of survival for victims of sudden cardiac arrest is directly related to how soon CPR is begun. Failure to successfully implement CPR promptly may result in permanent damage to the brain and other organs.

Catheter. A catheter is a hollow tube introduced into the body to drain fluid or to establish a canal. There are many types of catheters which can be made of metal, glass, hard or soft rubber, rubberized silk or plastic. A patient may have one or more catheters in place at a time.

Electrocardiogram. An instrument which measures the rate and rhythm of heartbeats. Commonly known as an EKG or cardiac strip.

Electroencephalography. A recording and analysis of the electrical activity of the brain. Commonly referred to as an EEG.

Foley Catheter. A tube inserted into the bladder to remove urine. Commonly known as a Foley cath, catheter, or Foley tube.

Gastrostomy tube. A tube inserted into the stomach for liquid feeding. Also known as a G-tube or GT-tube.

Intravenous. A catheter inserted in a vein to permit a steady supply of fluids or medications. Also known as IVs or lines.

Kidney Dialysis. A mechanical apparatus which provides for the process of filtering impurities from the blood. Accesses from a surgically placed shunt in the arm. Also referred to as renal dialysis or dialysis.

Nasogastric tube. A flexible tube inserted through the nostrils to the stomach to drain the fluids or provide nutrition. Often referred to as a NG tube.

Peritoneal Dialysis. Permits the filtering of impurities from the blood. Accesses through a surgically implanted tube in the abdominal cavity. Also known as P.D. or dialysis.

Tracheotomy. A surgical incision in the wind pipe often employed for long term ventilator use. Commonly referred to as a trache.

Ventilator. Apparatus used to mechanically breathe for the patient. Also known as a respirator or vent.

Many of these life-sustaining treatments are frequently used in conjunction with one another. One might be resuscitated, receive a tracheotomy, be placed on a respirator, fed, medicated and have waste removed through a series of tubes and catheters. Thereafter, the patient might be removed from such assistance and continue to live a normal life.

In addition to the technological references, one must also understand other terms and conditions that have both medical and legal implications. These terms, like the technological references, should be discussed with a medical professional. They should also be discussed with legal counsel and possibly incorporated in your Living Will. Please note that the following terms may be of varying significance or definition from one state to another.

Adult. An individual 18 years of age or older.

Attending Physician. The physician of choice, or one assigned to a given patient, who has the primary responsibility for treatment and care.

Comatose. There are varying levels of a comatose state, which generally refers to the deepest, most severe level of a condition, where the patient maintains neurological functions but has no cognitive ability. There is no awareness of the environment and the patient may be unresponsive to stimuli.

Death. Believe it or not, there are various forms of recognized death. "Clinical death" occurs when there are no independent heartbeats or breathing, however, some brain activity may remain as confirmed by an EEG. "Brain death" is based on purely neurological criteria occurring when the absence of brain activity is confirmed.

Decision-making capacity. For the purpose of Living Wills, this term loosely translates into competency. It refers to a patient's ability to understand and appreciate the nature and consequences of his or her healthcare decisions. This includes understanding and appreciating the benefits and risks of each alternative to proposed or existing healthcare methods.

Dementia. Refers to a progressive and irreversible loss of memory and cognitive functions.

"Do Not Resuscitate" order. Refers to a physician's written order not to attempt cardio-pulmonary resuscitation when and in the event the patient suffers a cardiac or respiratory arrest.

Life-sustaining treatment. This term references the use of any medical device, procedure, drugs, surgery, therapy and any mechanical or artificial means utilized to sustain, restore or replace a vital bodily function and thereby increase the life-span of the patient. It is important to note that there continues to be debate as to whether artificially provided fluids and nutrition should be considered as life-sustaining treatment in the same way that an apparatus such as a respirator may. You should refer to your state statute and attorney on this important issue.

Permanently unconscious. Refers to a condition where there has been a total and irreversible loss of consciousness and capacity for interaction with the environment. This commonly includes what is referred to as a persistent vegetative state or irreversible coma.

Terminal condition. Is defined as the final stage of an irreversible and fatal illness, disease or condition. A specific determination of life expectancy is not necessarily required as a diagnostic pre-condition. Terminal condition has also been defined as one which will result in death despite available medical care or when life-sustaining treatment merely postpones death. This definition is of extreme importance and may vary from one jurisdiction to another. It is necessary to confirm your understanding of this term in your state.

Vegetative State. A prolonged comatose state in which the patient has lost the functional portion of the brain that controls interaction with the environment and the cognitive process. In this condition, the patient may be able to maintain blood pressure, swallow, blink, and make certain noises. Some vegetative functions may operate but not independently. For example, there may be a need for assistance in breathing by way of a respirator.

Beyond the terminology, the reader must also understand there frequently are significant complicating factors when a patient is bedridden or incapacitated. Secondary infections stemming from the utilization of some life-sustaining measures are common. Also, bed sores, muscle atrophy, severe weight loss and restriction of movement often accompany later stages of the more serious illnesses or conditions.

A detailed study of all medical conditions and hospital policies are beyond the scope and purpose of this book. What has been written is more a framework for discussing and understanding the many issues associated with the execution of the Living Will. Any of your concerns regarding medical treatment or conditions should be discussed with a physician or other healthcare professional.

In discussing your Living Will with a doctor, your medical history and that of your family should be addressed and perhaps referenced in the document.

Your doctor will also assist you in understanding what the final stages of life may be like under certain circumstances. Your physician's affiliation with any hospital or healthcare institution should also be discussed to determine their policy on these matters.

Included in this book is a brief review of what certain religious faiths have stated with regard to Living Wills. Of course, the moral and religious implications, like the medical treatment and conditions, should be resolved through discussions with those on whom we depend for such guidance. To that end, the inclusion of those materials is also for the purpose of stimulating thought and advising that certain groups have made specific conclusions, largely in support of the Living Will concept.

As you would confer with the appropriate professional regarding a medical or religious concern, any outstanding legal questions with regard to your Living Will should be discussed with an attorney. There may be subtle but quite meaningful changes you wish to include in your Living Will that do not exist in a pre-printed form. Your Living Will must be explicit, properly executed and distributed. It must conform to your state Living Will statute where applicable. An attorney knowledgeable in this area will ensure your wishes are properly recorded, made known and acceded to.

These and other terms and conditions should also be discussed with your family and surrogate decision-maker if one has been named or is permitted. The more familiar you become with these concepts, the greater your sense of comfort and control will be through this planning process. Should you choose to have a healthcare representative, make certain he or she understands your wishes and will abide by them should the circumstances so require.

CHAPTER 3

CASE STUDIES

State and federal courts and legislatures have recently been active in making decisions and setting policy regarding the withholding or withdrawal of life-sustaining medical treatment for incompetent, unconscious and terminally ill patients.

The courts have traditionally been presented with competing interests and thereby required to discern the unstated intentions of those who have fallen ill. For example, a family member, hospital or appointed guardian might each be attempting to persuade the court regarding the patient's health care. It has been the court's responsibility to determine what the wishes of the uncommunicative or incompetent patient are. A Living Will, or "Advance Directive" as it is also referred to, will greatly reduce the necessity of searching for previously stated intentions or the possibility of them being mistaken or confused.

Karen Ann Quinlan, Respiratory Arrest

A lead case was decided by the New Jersey Supreme Court on March 31, 1976. In that matter, Karen Ann Quinlan, a New Jersey resident and young adult, for reasons still unclear, stopped breathing for at least two fifteen-minute periods on the night of April 15, 1975. Upon arrival at the hospital, she was totally unresponsive.

Soon after, Karen was diagnosed as being comatose. It was concluded that she had suffered from a prolonged lack of oxygen in the bloodstream. Karen remained unconscious, was given a tracheotomy, and had to be placed on a respirator.

Over time, Karen's condition improved from an initial sleep-like unresponsive state to where she would, at times, cry out. She remained, however, unaware of anyone or anything around her. Karen was in what is considered a chronic and persistent vegetative state, but she was not brain dead. As such, Karen's neurological condition impaired her ability to breathe.

Attempts to remove her from the respirator were unsuccessful. It was not known how long she would live without a respirator, but there was a strong likelihood that death would follow soon after its removal. The vegetative function of the brain, controlling bodily functions such as reaction to light and sound, blinking of eyes, and chewing, remained.

Karen required twenty-four-hour care by a team of four nurses and was fed through a nasogastric tube. She lost a great amount of weight and became emaciated. Her posture became fetal-like with extreme rigidity of the arms, legs and joints. Karen's doctors concluded that there was no form of treatment that could cure or improve her condition and that she could never again interact with the outside world.

This was Karen's situation, in part, when her father made application to the courts to be named guardian for his daughter. He sought the express power to authorize the discontinuance of all extraordinary procedures for sustaining his daughter's life, including the removal of the respirator.

In reviewing the father's request, the court considered many factors. It noted the high degree of love within the Quinlan home and that the father had spent intense and thoughtful months in coming to the conclusion that he must seek withdrawal of the life-supportive measures that kept his daughter alive.

The court first concluded that Karen's father would be permitted to assert his daughter's constitutional rights since she was incompetent to do so. The court noted that we enjoy a Right to Privacy under the Federal and New Jersey State Constitutions which could, under the appropriate circumstances, entitle her to the relief sought.

The court then had to balance Karen's Right to Privacy, as expressed through her father, with the state's interest in preserving the sanctity of human life. The court held that the state's interest weakened, and Karen's Right to Privacy increased as her condition worsened. As she suffered in a continuing and an unrelenting fashion, the ability to find impediments to her father's requests diminished.

In Karen's circumstances, it was clear to the court that her removal from the respirator should be permitted. The court held that since her Right to Privacy would permit termination of treatment under the circumstances, her ensuing death would not be homicide, but rather death brought about by existing natural causes.

Claire C. Conroy, Progressive Debilitation

Another New Jersey case of great importance involved an elderly woman named Claire C.

Conroy. In that case, Miss Conroy's nephew sought permission to remove a nasogastric feeding tube from his 84-year-old aunt who was bedridden and suffered from serious and irreversible physical and mental impairments. Miss Conroy was then residing in a nursing home.

In 1979, Miss Conroy was struggling with an ailment that resulted in her being disoriented and physically dependent. She was hospitalized on two separate occasions for dehydration and urinary tract infection and had developed gangrenous ulcers on her foot. It was during the second hospital stay that the nasogastric tube which extended from her nose through her esophagus and to her stomach was inserted. This was necessary because Miss Conroy was not eating adequately. Her medicines and food were given to her through this tube. When the tube was removed and she was hand fed, she was unable to consume sufficient amounts of nutrition to sustain herself and the tube had to be reinserted.

By the time the nephew went to court, Miss Conroy was confined to bed and unable to move from a semi-fetal position. She suffered from heart disease, hypertension, and diabetes. Her left leg was gangrenous to the knee and she had bed sores on her foot, leg and hip. A urinary catheter was in place. She could not control her bowels or speak.

In certain ways, however, Miss Conroy did interact with her environment. She had minimal movement in her limbs. She could scratch herself and pulled at her bandages, the tubes and catheter. She moaned occasionally when moved or when bandages were changed. Her eyes sometimes followed movement within the room and she smiled when her hair was combed or while receiving a comforting rub.

There was testimony that Miss Conroy was not brain dead, comatose, or in a chronic vegetative state. Rather, her intellectual capacity was extremely limited and she would never improve. It could not be determined whether she was capable of experiencing pain.

It was agreed that if the nasogastric tube were removed, Miss Conroy would die of dehydration in about one week. It was testified that the result of this would be painful, as would her death. The Court was to base its decision upon the conclusion that Miss Conroy would likely die within one year even if treatment were continued.

This is clearly an agonizing and difficult decision to make. As this passage was read, you must have wondered what the court's decision would be. If you were a judge, what would you decide? Certainly there was suffering and a great loss of function. This would possibly weigh in favor of discontinuing treatment. But consider the eye movement, scratching and smile when being comforted. Certainly death is not far away, but should that be of any consequence? If so, why should the decision not be to give more comforting rubs than to terminate life-sustaining treatment?

The difficulty of this decision would certainly be compounded if the patient were your parent, spouse or child as opposed to a person whose name you know only in print. This, for many, is perhaps the most compelling reason to have a Living Will.

The court stated that these tragic situations raise disturbing questions that are difficult to answer:

> *"As scientific advances make it possible for us to live longer than ever before, even when most of our physical and mental capacities have been irrevocably lost, patients and their families are increasingly asserting a right to die a natural death without undue dependence on medical technology or unnecessarily protracted agony, in short, a right to die with dignity."* 4

In the court's legal analysis, the right of a person to control his or her own body was acknowledged as a basic societal understanding, long recognized under the law. The Court again stated that this opportunity was also protected by an individual's Right to Privacy embodied in the United States Constitution. These rights are not absolute, however, as they must be weighed against the interests of preserving life, preventing suicide, safeguarding the integrity of the medical profession, and protecting innocent third parties.

As in Karen Ann Quinlan's case, the court decided that if Miss Conroy were competent, she could have chosen to have the nasogastric tube withdrawn.

It was further decided that an institutionalized elderly person, regardless of his or her physical and mental limitations or life expectancy, has the same right to receive medical treatment as a competent young person who is fully functional. Miss Conroy, unlike Karen, was awake and conscious and interacted with her environment to a limited extent despite her severe and permanent impairment and short life expectancy. The Court was aware that

> *"Large numbers of aged, chronically ill, institutionalized persons fall within this general category."* [5]

The court also held that under circumstances such as these, life-sustaining treatment may be withheld or withdrawn when it is clear a particular patient would have refused the treatment. The court then noted that a patient's wishes might be embodied in a Living Will. The question remained, however, of what should be done when the patient had never fully expressed his or her desires regarding life-sustaining treatment.

It was decided that life-sustaining treatment could be withheld or withdrawn under such circumstances where there is at least some trustworthy evidence that the patient would have refused the treatment and it is clear to the surrogate decision-maker that the burdens of the patient's continued life with the treatment outweigh the benefits of life sustained thereby. The court envisioned a patient who is suffering in unavoidable pain and will continue so for the rest of his or her life, and that these burdens outweigh the physical pleasure, emotional enjoyment, or moral and intellectual satisfaction that may be derived from life.

In the event that there is a lack of evidence with regard to what the patient might have wished, the court held that life-sustaining treatment might still be withheld or withdrawn from a patient under similar circumstances. This would occur when the burdens of treatment clearly and markedly outweigh the benefits that he or she derives from life. Further, the recurring, unavoidable and severe pain of the patient's life with treatment must be such that the administration of life-sustaining treatment would be inhumane.

The court acknowledged, however, that even in the case of severe pain, life-sustaining treatment should never be withdrawn from one who had previously expressed the desire to be kept alive. The court warned that it did not authorize anyone to make a decision discontinuing life-sustaining treatment for another based upon an assessment of the value, worth or social utility of the patient's life. Simply stated, no one should be given the authority to say that another's life is not worth living.

The court remained cautious and stated further that, whenever a patient's wishes are not clear, it is best to err, if at all, in favor of preserving life.

Another distinction often asserted, that being the difference between withholding and withdrawing life-sustaining treatment, was addressed next. Some have argued that discontinuing life-sustaining treatment is an act of taking a life and is therefore more offensive than the passive act of omitting treatment. The argument continues that we are not morally obligated to help one another, but we are obligated not to interfere with another's life-sustaining routines.

The court responded that whether necessary treatment is withheld or withdrawn, the consequence, that being death, is the same. It was reasoned that if one were to permit the withholding, but not the withdrawal of life-sustaining treatment, medical providers might be discouraged from attempting certain types of care which could not later be withdrawn.

Next the court dealt with the issue of whether there existed a distinction between termination of artificial feeding and hydration and other forms of life-sustaining medical treatment, such as a respirator. The Court stated that artificial feedings by way of nasogastric tubes, gastrostomies and intravenous infusions are medical procedures utilized to compensate for a physical dysfunction. These treatments carry their own risks and side effects. A feeding tube is similar to a respirator in that both are artificial means of prolonging life when the body is unable to do so. Feeding tubes may lead to pneumonia, nasal, throat, stomach and other internal irritations, and general discomfort. This may often require placement of restraints on the patient to prevent him or her from removing the tubes. Finally, withholding nutrition or fluids through the removal or denial of feeding or hydration devices would result in death which may be no more painful than that induced by the removal of other medical treatments. The court even considered observations that one not receiving nourishment may be more comfortable in death than patients in comparable situations who are being artificially fed and hydrated.

The Quinlan court decided that the concurrence of the patient's guardian, family, attending physician, and hospital prognosis committee was required to terminate life-sustaining treatment. The court in Claire Conroy's case, however, held that these decision-making procedures were not appropriate for one confined to a nursing home.

At the time, the average age of nursing home residents was 82 years. Most suffered from chronic and debilitating medical problems including mental impairments. The court recognized that the vast majority of patients who enter nursing homes will eventually die there and that nursing home residents are often without any surviving family. Thus, they are frequently isolated and remain unvisited. The patient is less frequently contacted by a physician as doctors were found to often avoid nursing homes. As a result, the court decided that when faced with the question of withholding or withdrawing life-sustaining treatment from an elderly and incompetent nursing home resident, other state agencies and medical personnel must be involved.

These observations of nursing homes and personnel were the court's and do not necessarily reflect this writer's opinion.

Miss Conroy died before the matter was heard by the New Jersey Supreme Court, but the case was considered because of the issue's importance. Significantly, the court stated, "Perhaps most important, this decision may encourage individuals to use living wills."6

The Conroy case epitomizes the intellectual, moral and emotional contortions a decision-maker must go through to rationalize and balance competing considerations, all in an effort to do nothing more than what the stroke of a pen upon a Living Will might accomplish. Without an Advance Directive, the surrogate decision-maker can do little more than estimate what the intentions of the patient might have been. If none were ever stated, a judgment on substituted criteria may occur. The best a surrogate decision-maker can do then is to guess correctly.

Nancy Ellen Jobes, Nursing Home Resident

In the matter of Nancy Ellen Jobes, decided on January 24, 1987, also by the Supreme Court for the State of New Jersey, it was determined that facilities caring for persons such as Ms. Jobes and Miss Conroy could not refuse to participate in the withdrawal of life-sustaining treatment. It was reasoned that a family should not surrender the right to choose among different medical alternatives when a member is placed in a nursing home. A person may not be deprived of his or her constitutional rights solely by being a resident of such a facility. This conclusion might have been different if the nursing home had made it known, prior to admission, that it would not participate in the withholding or withdrawal of such treatment. This should remain a consideration when choosing a healthcare facility or physician.

Elizabeth Visbeck, Stroke Victim

Not all cases reviewed by the courts have resulted in the withholding or removal of life-sustaining measures. In the matter of Elizabeth Visbeck, the courts were faced with the question of whether a feeding tube should be surgically implanted in the stomach of an elderly woman who was severely disabled by a stroke.

Elizabeth suffered a stroke on November 8, 1985, resulting in a loss of much of her mental capacity and paralysis of the right side. She was left, among other things, unable to speak, walk, or swallow.

Shortly after suffering the stroke, a nasogastric feeding tube was inserted. Due to complications, the tube was removed and could not thereafter be reinserted. It was then determined that intravenous feeding was necessary.

It was accepted that a patient in Elizabeth's condition may survive on intravenous to the extent that serious dehydration can be prevented. However, the intravenous would be insufficient to meet the minimum daily caloric needs of the patient. This results in a nutritional deficit and loss of body weight. Approximately one month of this deficiency would be critical and result in death. Additionally, the intravenous would have the effect of wearing out the patient's veins, resulting in her inability to absorb the feeding. Within approximately one month, the veins would no longer be able to handle the intravenous.

Because the nasogastric feeding tube could not be reinserted, the attending physicians felt that it was necessary to implant a feeding tube in the stomach. They characterized the surgery as uncomplicated and, due to Elizabeth's incompetency, a relative's consent was sought. The consent was denied. Elizabeth's son felt that this would prolong his mother's suffering.

The court ordered the immediate implantation of the feeding tube. This was done despite the fact that there was no prior statement, oral or written, of what the patient would like to have done under the circumstances.

The court reasoned that, in spite of all the problems that Elizabeth suffered from, she maintained some awareness of her surroundings and was able to react to them at a meaningful level. She saw movement and noticed when people entered the room. She had been observed adjusting her blanket and appeared to respond to an extended hand by grasping it. The sounds she made were unintelligible but were not mere moans or groans. It was reported that she had stated distinct words or phrases, had given answers to questions, and was also capable of feeling pain.

Under these circumstances and where there was not a clear statement of the patient's wishes with regard to future care, the court rendered its decision requiring treatment. The court, however, left open the question and possibility that the tube could be removed at a later date upon a change in Elizabeth's condition.

Kathleen Farrel, Nervous System Disorder

One of the state's interests which must be balanced against a patient's request to withhold or terminate treatment is the protection of innocent third parties. In the matter of Kathleen Farrell, the court dealt with an objection made by a guardian appointed for Mrs. Farrell's children. The guardian objected to Kathleen's request to be removed from a respirator. Mrs. Farrell had two teenage children. In 1982, she experienced a nervous system disorder that results in degeneration of the body's muscles. There is no available treatment or cure. Once afflicted, one is left without the potential of movement yet without impairment of his or her mental faculties. Life expectancy is limited to one to three years even with the use of life-sustaining treatment. Mrs. Farrell was required to have a tracheotomy and be connected to a respirator.

In 1985, Mrs. Farrell told her husband that she wished to be disconnected from her respirator. It was concluded that she was not suffering from a clinically depressed state and needed no psychiatric treatment. She was advised that she would die if taken from the respirator and it was further concluded that her decision was informed, voluntary and made by a competent, though physically ill individual. Mrs. Farrell was described as a woman who had lost more than one-third of her body weight, had no control of her limbs or bowels, and had difficulty swallowing. She was attended by nurses twenty-four hours a day. She could see but had difficulty talking. She expressed emotions, felt pain, but was given medication to alleviate it. When asked why she wished to have the respirator disconnected, she responded, "I'm tired of suffering." 7

The court restated the accepted rule that a competent adult has the right to decline or discontinue medical treatment, but the right to refuse is not absolute. It was then decided that there were no interests greater than Mrs. Farrell's including those of her children. It was noted that Mrs. Farrel was not disregarding her children's interests but had partially based her decision on the extreme stress under which they had lived. Additionally, she knew that the children would continue to be cared for by Mr. Farrell. The court then set guidelines for discontinuing life-support treatment for a competent patient who is living at home.

It is most unfortunate that Mrs. Farrell, as Claire Conroy, died before the court rendered its decision. However, this underscores the obvious problem which exists when a patient's wishes are subject to competing points of view. For example, a relative, guardian, and healthcare institution may each have an opportunity to be heard by the court. In the event that they are unsatisfied, they may appeal the decision to a higher court.

This exacts an enormous amount of resources and creates a level of heightened stress and anxiety for friends, family and the sufferer far beyond that which would otherwise accompany the patient's weakened mental and physical state.   For one who wishes to die peacefully and naturally, time slips away, as do the rights to privacy and self-determination.

William Bartling, Medical Emergency

In another case, that of William Francis Bartling, the Califonia courts were forced to decide whether a competent adult patient with a serious and probably incurable, but non-terminal illness, had the right over the objection of his physicians and hospital to have life-sustaining equipment removed where its withdrawal would result in his death.

William was an elderly gentleman who initially entered a facility for treatment of his depression. During a physical examination, it was learned that a tumor existed in his chest area. While taking a biopsy of the tumor, a needle punctured his lung and caused it to collapse. Tubes were inserted in his chest and nasal passages. However, due to an emphysema condition, the damage caused by the biopsy needle did not heal and the lung would not reinflate. William was thereafter given a tracheotomy and placed on a respirator. Efforts to remove him from these life-support systems were unsuccessful.

On numerous occasions, William apparently attempted to disconnect the ventilator and remove tubes. The institution responded by placing restraints on his wrists. The facility refused to remove the ventilator or restraints despite requests from William and his wife.

William had apparently signed a simple form of Living Will. The Living Will was accompanied by a declaration that requested the removal of life-sustaining treatment and a Durable Power of Attorney appointing his wife as a proxy healthcare decision-maker. Additionally, the court was provided with William's video-taped testimony in which he expressed a wish to be removed from the ventilator by nodding and shaking his head, as he could no longer speak.

The court decided that the right to have life-support equipment disconnected was not limited to comatose and terminally ill patients. The court stated further that California had long since recognized the legal right one has to control his or her own medical treatment. William's constitutional rights were recognized then weighed against the competing interests as discussed in previous cases.

The court quickly dispatched any notion that removal of the ventilator was equivalent to assisting in a suicide. It was reasoned that the removal of the ventilator would merely hasten the inevitable death which would result from natural causes. Most significantly, the court noted that in the absence of a statute stating otherwise, there existed no legal requirement that judicial approval was necessary before the decision to withdraw treatment could be made. This was a ruling which had been made elsewhere but was not universally accepted.

The nightmarish quality of the treatment received by William Bartling, highlighted by his lung being punctured and finding himself thereafter being placed under restraints, is deepened by the irony of his death which occurred the afternoon before his matter was heard by the court.

Selma Saunders, Emphysema & Lung Cancer

A most interesting case dealing specifically with the enforceability of a Living Will was decided by the Supreme Court for the State of New York. Selma Saunders was 70 years old and suffered from emphysema and lung cancer. She was administered oxygen continually and her condition was progressive and without the likelihood of cure.

Selma requested the court to determine if her Living Will would be enforceable in the State of New York and operable without the requirement of further court involvement. New York did not have a statute permitting or requiring the recognition of Living Wills. Unlike many other cases which have been discussed, this application to the court was actually premature. The court considered the matter, however, due to its public importance and the danger of courts being repeatedly too late to provide relief.

The court stated that it could not declare the Living Will legally binding as that was the responsibility of the legislature. Also noted were some of the inherent weaknesses of the Durable Power of Attorney, including the requirement that there be a third party or surrogate decision-maker to act on behalf of the sufferer which is what Selma specifically attempted to avoid through her Living Will.

Selma's writing was accepted, however, as a statement of her informed consent to medical treatment and her authorization of refusal or discontinuation of certain medical treatment. This cleared the way for a granting of her wishes without further need for court intervention.

Most notably, the court stated that the Living Will is:

> "... *evidence of the most persuasive quality and is a clear and convincing demonstration that while competent the petitioner clearly and explicity expressed an informed, rational and knowing decision. . . and it should be given great weight by the hospital*

authorities and treating physicians attending her." [8]

Tucked away within the court's opinion was a claim that it did not endorse the choice of death over life. Rather the court attempted to:

"...recognize that there is truly a distinction between curing the ill and comforting and easing the dying, and permitting death to come in a natural, dignified and peaceful manner, where that is the sacred, rational, knowing wish of a terminally ill patient." [9]

The significance of the case is that the courts clearly appear ready and willing to permit individuals to control their own medical destinies and when necessary will work very hard at assuring this through creative legal analysis.

An Innocent Victim of Crime

Another interesting case citing the courts' predisposition to the validity and utility of Living Wills arose during a criminal trial in the District of Columbia. In that case, an 85-year-old woman was the victim of a purse-snatching that resulted in her falling and receiving injuries to the extent that she required life-sustaining treatment, including a respirator. The criminal defendant objected to being found guilty of murder when his victim died.

The convicted purse-snatcher argued his victim's death was not a result of the assault, but rather was caused by an improper cessation of life-sustaining treatment without judicial approval. The court rejected this argument, stating that there is no requirement that the judiciary intervene prior to life-sustaining treatment being withdrawn pursuant to a Living Will.

Nancy Cruzan, Car Accident Victim

Most recently, the United States Supreme Court handed down a decision in the matter of Nancy Cruzan. In January, 1983, Nancy lost control of her car, resulting in an accident from which she apparently suffered a loss of oxygen. After being rushed to the hospital, she never regained consciousness. Soon after, she was placed on life-sustaining treatment which included being given nutrition through a gastrostomy tube. Nancy remained in a persistent vegetative state through 1987, when her parents asked that the tube be removed. Nancy, who was 25 years old when the accident occurred, had no Living Will. Her parents were left to argue their understanding of what Nancy's wishes would have been. A friend also gave testimony regarding recollections she had of statements Nancy made while competent.

Before the matter reached the United States Supreme Court, the Missouri Supreme Court had ruled that Nancy's tube feeding must be continued indefinitely as there was an absence of "clear and convincing" evidence that she would have wanted otherwise. The United States Supreme Court affirmed the decision by agreeing that states may require such a high standard of evidence and apparently sealed Nancy's fate to remain connected to life-sustaining apparatus.

The court did, however, acknowledge a competent individual's constitutional right to refuse life-sustaining treatment and, significantly, made no legal distinction between artificially provided nutrition and other life-sustaining measures. Finally, the case may be read to confirm that individuals who provide "clear and convincing" evidence of their wishes, perhaps through a Living Will, will have them constitutionally protected.

The parents' request to have Nancy removed from the feeding and hydration tubes was later permitted due to additional evidence regarding her wishes. Nancy died within two weeks of the removal.

The Cruzan decision leaves a mixed legacy. We have learned that requests from family, even when accompanied by other evidence, may not be sufficient and treatment might be ordered to continue for an indefinite period. We also learned, however, that if one's intentions are clearly and convincingly stated, they will likely be upheld by the highest court in the land. With that understanding, the only question remaining is: What would be the best way to clearly and convincingly state one's wishes? The answer is obvious -- through a carefully drafted and properly executed Living Will.

Beyond the Horizon

The balancing act required by society to reconcile medical and technological advances with what is traditionally a more static concept of human dignity does not begin or end with questions regarding continued medical care for the elderly, incompetent or those with slight life expectancies. As we have seen, one who is competent yet in an extremely debilitated physical condition may refuse or order withdrawal of life-sustaining treatment. Persons who are mentally competent and physically debilitated, though not diagnosed as suffering from a terminal disease, may also be permitted to have life-sustaining treatment withheld or withdrawn.

The fear that the circumstances when life-sustaining measures can be withheld or withdrawn may expand even further is maintained by some of the very few detractors of the Living Will. Their arguments include the assertion that any withholding or withdrawal of medical treatment represents another step down a very slippery slope of respect for human life and its preservation at all costs.

This fear is not wholly without an emotional, if not a rational basis. This concern, however, is more an argument in favor of executing a Living Will than against its acceptance. Think about this for a moment. Remember that your Living Will may direct not only to withhold or withdraw treatment, but to demand the implementation and continuation of any such medical treatments that might be reasonably available and appropriate. If the Living Will movement is more an affront to personal integrity and less an expansion of individual rights, than those who affirmatively state the bodily protections and safeguards they desire are better protected.

An example of this is a phone call that I received from family members of an AIDS patient who were heartbroken with the advice their afflicted child had received from medical providers. It was alleged that they told the patient to opt out of future life-sustaining treatments as the condition was terminal and such measures would be futile.

This young person wanted to live as long as possible and hold on to whatever life had to offer, regardless of what that might entail. Maybe this was born out of the early confrontation with death, the patient's youth, or hope that a cure would be forthcoming. Perhaps it was just a strong love for life. Nevertheless, a patient has the right to be medically treated as he or she might reasonably request, and a Living Will may help ensure treatment if that is one's desire.

As an AIDS sufferer, this young person was part of a group or class of citizens that is clearly definable. This group shares many of the characteristics, such as a power base weakened through economics, demographics, and likely prejudice, of others who have previously been considered by the courts to require special attention to protect their rights, as they may be more likely than others to be singled out for unconstitutional and biased treatment.

It is not merely rhetorical to ask which class of citizens might be targeted next. Could it be the aged female nursing home resident who has not declared her wishes or intentions regarding life-sustaining treatment? Might it be the elderly person who has exhausted personal and insurance resources? Perhaps and perhaps not. The point to keep in mind is that your Living Will may be utilized to protect the likelihood of what each individual may describe as a natural and dignified death, be that through termination of life-sustaining treatment under certain circumstances or the continuation of all reasonable treatment for so long as possible and appropriate.

CHAPTER 4

THINGS TO CONSIDER

W hat you may sense, and accurately so, is that there are numerous competing interests which exist where the withholding or withdrawal of life-sustaining medical treatment is being considered. This is further complicated when there are no clear intentions expressed in a Living Will.

Surrogate Decision-Makers

In the event there is no Living Will, a surrogate decision-maker, either formally appointed and permitted by law or informally called upon by attending medical personnel, will necessarily need to consider serious moral, financial, religious and legal matters. Unfortunately, he or she may even perceive the decision to withhold or withdraw elements of life support as being the reason for or the actual cause of death. This concern is so real, it is recommended to healthcare professionals that:

> *"Specific treatment options for probable complications should be explored as early as possible to avoid unnecessary guilt in*

surrogates who are forced to decide for incompetent patients." 10

These are just a few of the considerations that cause debate as to whether a surrogate decision-maker should be named in a Living Will, if permitted, or by way of a Durable Power of Attorney.

The decision to withhold or withdraw life support becomes further complicated when there is disagreement among family members who are traditionally called upon to make such decisions on behalf of the patient. There may be as many opinions as there are relationships between the patient and family members. As you have discovered in the case studies, disagreement between interested parties may result in considerable legal battles, expenditures of financial and emotional resources, and the patient dying long before the resolution of his or her interests could be established by the courts.

This problem may reoccur during the treatment of a patient because a decision whether to initiate life support is only the first question. Once having risen to the occasion and made a decision to implement life-sustaining treatment, family members may next confront an even more emotionally trying dilemma, that being a decision as to whether treatment, once commenced, should be terminated. It is recognized that:

"...grief stricken or guilty family members may attempt to relieve their distress at the patient's expense by pressing for disproportionate treatment...that once an intervention is started, its withdrawal can cause problems." [11]

There can be no doubt that the issue of ending life support is not only emotionally difficult, but also confusing. The very technology that saved the patient's life is now, in some fashion, being used to terminate it. It has been stated that there is no difference between withholding and withdrawing treatment once it begins because both are means to the same end. [12] To some, however, there remains a significant difference between the two.

Today's Family

The opportunity to name a surrogate decision-maker in your Living Will or Durable Power of Attorney for Healthcare, or to continue without a Living Will, must be considered in light of changing demographics and the deterioration of what has been the traditional family unit. Statistics show that it is increasingly unlikely that family may be available to make decisions on another's behalf.

People are now more likely than ever to be living alone. This trend increased throughout the 1980s as single person households grew by 26%. Many younger people are living alone because they choose not to marry at earlier ages as was done in the past. During the 1950s, the average age of marriage was 20.1 years for women and 22.5 years for men. By the late 1980s, women were waiting until they were 23.6 years to marry and men until almost the age of 26. In fact, the 1990 census is projected to show that one in four households will be that of a single person, living alone. [13]

Although many agree that they would not wish their children or parents to be burdened with making a decision to withhold or withdraw life-sustaining treatment, many of us may not, presently or in the future, have a spouse to do so. Statistics again show that it is becoming more likely that many men and women will be maintaining families on their own without a spouse present.

Between 1970 and 1989, the number of families headed by men alone doubled to 2.8 million. The trend of women maintaining households on their own increased even more dramatically. Female-headed households rose 50% from 1950 to 1970 and 98% from 1970 to 1989. [14] Collectively, and on a statistical basis, all of us will not only have a somewhat limited chance of a spouse available to help make these decisions, but we will also have less of a likelihood of children being available to do so.

Since 1972, the birthrate has continued to be below replacement level. The average American family is smaller than it has ever been in history and has reached a point where there are only .96 children per family, down from 1.41 in 1960. [15]

All these factors become more important as we age, and sickness and the need for intensive healthcare becomes more likely. The probability of having a chronic illness increases with age.

"More than four out of five persons 65 and over have at least one chronic condition and multiple conditions are commonplace among older persons." [16]

Aging Trends

In our families, community, state and country, the concept of a Living Will has likely grown from an exercise in responsibility to a social and economic imperative. We must consider not only how each of us will be living when we are 65, but how the nation and its component generations will deal with our rapidly aging population.

Those who take a jaundiced view of Living Will legislation may point to the economic benefits of terminating life-sustaining treatment and suggest a relationship with the impending crises caused by spiraling healthcare costs and insurance concerns. Should there be such a benefit, it is likely ancillary and not what has driven this issue into law. In fact, Living Will statutes may expressly prohibit insurance carriers from conditioning continuation or approval of insurance upon execution of a Living Will.

The prospect of being left without a spouse or family member for the reasons stated increases with age. When younger, our chances of living alone are greatly influenced by choice, including whether or when to marry or divorce. Divorce impacted half of all couples married during the 1970s. [17] As we age, however, we find ourselves more likely to be widows or widowers. In 1988, almost 89% of widowed people, male and female, were over age 55. It is important to note that 83% of that widowed group were women. [18] It is also interesting to note that 40% of all women 65 and older live alone as compared to 16% of all men of the same age. During the decade of the 1980s, 30.4% of all men and women over 65 lived by themselves. [19]

Due in part to the disintegration of the nuclear family and the increased life expectancy of survivors of the marriage, many elderly do not remain with their families as they had in the past. This results in an increased need for a declaration in writing so that medical healthcare providers can, in the absence of family or similarly positioned persons, be made aware of one's wishes.

Special Concerns For Women

It is apparent that the issues of aging and medical care are especially important to women. Traditionally, people have thought that women are healthier than men at an older age. That trend, however, is changing:

> *"Over the past decade, concurrent with dramatic changes in lifestyle and social roles for women, mortality rates have shifted, resulting in a decreasing advantage for women."* [20]

Although women still outlive men, the last decade has shown a steady decline especially in those 45 years and older. Additionally, because women still live longer than men, there are some illnesses that are of a primary concern to the elderly woman.

A good example is Alzheimer's Disease. Because it most often strikes persons over 80 years of age, the majority of people who suffer from Alzheimer's are women. Unfortunately, Alzheimer's robs its victims of their mental faculties and in many cases as the disease progresses makes it impossible for them to make decisions. Cerebrovascular diseases, which may also make it difficult for people to communicate with clarity, also rank extremely high as a diagnosis for women over 65. [21]

Women also need to pay particular attention to the relationship which exists between them and the healthcare profession. For example, two-thirds of all surgical procedures in this country are performed on women. Also, inadequate access to quality healthcare and health insurance is more likely to affect women. [22] Women have a higher risk of being prescribed a wide range of sedative drugs and run more of a risk of becoming addicted or having an acute drug reaction. [23] Such circumstances are often cited as a cause for one's competency or decision-making ability being called into question. Finally, all of these problems may be further aggravated by a social setting in which financial and bureaucratic institutional settings are male dominated and oriented.

More People Live in Nursing Homes

The ripples continue to extend from the rapid advancement of medical technology, increased life expectancy, and changing family, interpersonal and societal relationships. Much of what has been discussed up to this point also demonstrates an increased probability that we may find ourselves needing to live in a nursing home. As painful as it is to consider, it is a good possibility that either upon entering a nursing home or at some time during the stay, one's ability to think clearly and make decisions about medical needs and options will decrease. In fact, 94% of the residents in nursing homes are said to have mental disorders. [24]

The trend toward nursing home living has been increasing and is expected to continue. It is projected that over a lifetime, the risk of entering a nursing home and spending a long period of time there is substantial. In 1964, little more than one-half million people were residing in nursing homes or professional care facilities. In 1985, that number of residents had almost tripled. In fact, it is projected that of those people who turned 65 in 1990, 43% will eventually enter a nursing home. [25]

As the likelihood of entering a nursing home increases with age, it is probable that of those in the age group of 65 to 74, 17% will enter a nursing home. Another 26% will enter between the ages of 75 to 84, and a dramatic rise to 60% will enter during the years of 85 to 94. [26]

The length of time any one of us will need to stay in a nursing home is likely to be considerable. Fifty-five percent will have a total lifetime use of at least one year. Twenty-one percent of those who enter a nursing home will have a total lifetime use of five or more years. 27

As you have read, the courts have acknowledged problems for the aged residing in nursing homes. Perhaps through no fault of the institutions, residents find themselves increasingly isolated. In addition, the nursing homes represent a level of bureaucracy and interest which can become cumbersome and amount to an additional barrier in having the patient's wishes acceded to.

As these demographic rings widen, they intersect with others and their wake can represent an acute class of persons who may be impacted by severe consequences. Again, the trend toward living alone greatly increases our chances of entering a nursing home as we grow older. Those living alone may not have a friend or family member to assist in making decisions in the event there is no Living Will. Hence, for this group, the need for a Living Will cannot be overstated.

Only slightly more than one-quarter of those persons who were married at the time of their deaths had used nursing homes as opposed to two-fifths of those who are single due to death, divorce, separation from a spouse, or who had never been married at the time of death. The association between the amount of time spent in nursing homes and marital status is even more striking.

> *"Of those persons who have entered a nursing home, 7% who were married when they died resided there for five or more years. This compares to 16% of those who were widowed, 17% who were separated or divorced, and 29% who had never been married."* [28]

Women also run a higher risk of entering a nursing home and spending longer periods of time as a resident. According to projections, almost two out of every three persons who use nursing home care will be women as will nearly eight of every ten persons spending at least five years as a resident in such a facility. [29]

Unexpected Hospital Admissions

Hospital admissions represent another area of concern for those wishing to maintain control over the type and duration of medical treatment, as many such admissions are of an urgent nature. Such admissions may immediately place the patient in the position of receiving life-sustaining treatment and care.

Also to be considered is another dynamic which is reported to exist in the medical institutions. The New England Journal of Medicine states that:

> *"Too often, life sustaining measures are instituted in the intensive care unit without sufficient thought to the proper goals of treatment...there is a bias in the intensive care unit toward continuing aggressive measures that may be inappropriate."* [30]

A Spectrum of Perspectives

We see then that there is a wealth of information which must be considered when deciding whether one should execute a Living Will and, if so, what it may direct. Beyond relying upon one's own intuition and conviction, many groups and organizations have taken positions upon the issue thereby rendering guidance to those considering the question.

Because the question is perceived by many as fraught with moral and ethical concerns, it may be helpful to consider the position on Living Wills taken by some organized communities of faith.

The Catholic Church expresses no disfavor with the concept in general, however, it has stated particular concerns regarding its breadth. Those concerns center on the withholding or withdrawal of artificially provided fluids and nutrition and the impact a decision to terminate life-sustaining treatment may have upon one who is pregnant.

The Church focuses a great deal of attention on the withholding or withdrawal of artificially provided fluids and nutrition as it maintains that, in certain circumstances, this would initiate a new cause of death through starvation or dehydration. The position appears to be that the withholding or withdrawal of nutrition or hydration should not be permitted in the event that those factors, rather than the underlying illness or injury, would be the sole or principal cause of the patient's death.

With regard to a patient who may be pregnant but otherwise existing under circumstances where a Living Will would be operative, the Church feels that there should not be a withholding or withdrawal of life-sustaining treatment.

Sectors within the Jewish faith appear to have recognized the usefulness of the Living Will and believe that the patient maintains a fairly large area of autonomy with regard to his or her treatment. However, any such decisions must be exercised within the guidelines established by Jewish law.

The United Methodist Church has expressed the belief that one may die with dignity, loving care, and without effort to prolong terminal illness merely because the technology is available to do so. In a joint statement with the Roman Catholic Church, it was made clear that decisions which subordinate the humane dying of a terminally ill person to the technological imperative is inconsistent with Christian values and traditions. Further, individuals are encouraged to be active participants in medical treatment decisions and to stipulate for their future care through written directives.

The Episcopal Church has resolved to recognize and approve a beneficial document to be used by its members as a vehicle for expressing wishes pertaining to medical treatment when one is incompetent to do so.

Each of these religious bodies expresses a concern for maintaining and encouraging the support and participation of the family and religious community in these decision-making processes. Aside from considering a specific religion's stated position and one's own intuitive and carefully considered opinion, a review of the medical community's perspective, which has often expressed support for the Living Will, may be helpful. Assuming that the patient's illness is terminal, he or she does not have very long to live, and requests have been made clear,

"...life-at-all-costs heroics" and "Overtreat-ment of the terminally ill strikes physicians as both wasteful and inhumane. And patients living within sight of death also of-ten find themselves more concerned with the quality of life that remains than with its quantity. Once reconciled to the inevitable, they want to die with dignity, not tethered to a battery of machines in an intensive-care unit like a laboratory specimen under glass."[31]

Although many of these comments have dealt with the demographic profile of the elderly, a Living Will is an opportunity which should be taken advantage of by any adult who has had the time and inclination to seriously plan his or her future.

Many young adults and middle-aged persons have taken this most responsible step toward maintaining autonomy and lifting burdens from their family and loved ones. A larger number of elderly are actively planning their future medical care through Living Wills. Perhaps it is the reality of aging which moves the speculative discussion from the kitchen table or cocktail party to active solicitation of professionals and the execution of documents.

Ironically, younger and middle-aged adults will sometimes urge, prod and pay for such life planning on behalf of their parents but neglect doing so for themselves. Is there any rational basis for this? Of course not, as we all face the same eventuality and the possibility of unexpected emergency medical care.

If there is a disproportionate concern among the elderly for planning of this nature, including a Living Will, it may be simply that they have acquired a better understanding of life and its values than younger generations.

CHAPTER 5

THINKING ELDERLY

Successful aging has been said to include one's ability to cope with the changes life is offering and the adaptation to the resulting and unfamiliar situations one is confronted with. This includes not only the fears of pain and inconvenience associated with illness, but also the social and psychological consequences of loss of autonomy, productivity and economic security. To ease the transition into older life, one does not need to do anything new. He or she may simply continue with those mechanisms for coping and adjusting that have proven successful in the past. 32

One such coping mechanism is planning. The type of planning we are concerned with here is the Living Will. It is the design and intention, in part, for a Living Will to reduce the stress, fear, and anxiety associated with the medical and physical aspects of aging.

Unfortunately, and incorrectly, disease and dying are all too often associated with old age. This is not suprising when we consider that presently, more than two-thirds of all deaths occur in institutional settings, generally in hospitals and nursing homes. [33]

The association of death with the aged is obviously no fault of the elderly. Modern science and technology has made death an event more likely to occur at the end of the natural life-span. Many of those who might have died from childhood disease or during midlife from sickness or trauma, are now saved from death and live to an older age through vaccination, medication and quality emergency healthcare.

A healthy elderly person is no closer to death than a healthy person of lesser years. The frequency in death may be different, but its character remains unchanged. Illness and death are blind to age.

This is an appropriate time to note that, because data accumulated on a grand scale is generalized in nature, there is a risk of insensitivity to the individual. This can often be as dehumanizing and tending towards callousness as the technology we attempt to manage through a Living Will. With that in mind, we must remember that each statistic referenced or trend discussed represents one or more lives: Mothers, fathers, sisters, brothers, grandparents, children, spouses, and neighbors. By focusing on the individual, we are reminded that a Living Will is an intimate and personal expression.

The wishes and intentions it contains may be as unique as the individuals affixing their name to it.

When deciding upon the type and nature of directives embodied in a Living Will, great care should be given to permitting the elderly to make their own choices. Through the life process, the elderly may have acquired a perspective which time has yet to allow someone more youthful to acquire. Just as it would be unfair to expect children to begin their lives and experience the world based upon adult standards and perceptions, so it is inappropriate for an elder to have the end of his or her life orchestrated by one more youthful who does not share the same fears, concerns, anticipations and expectations.

Children may certainly have a role to play in the Living Will process and planning for future medical treatment for parents, grandparents and similarly situated loved ones. However, that role is not to dictate, but rather to initiate discussion, advise of opportunities and suggest consideration of issues.

To assist and better understand the elderly, a discussion of certain concerns and myths is helpful. First and foremost, remember that the physically and mentally healthy senior, in most instances, has the capacity for making decisions of the type and nature that are embodied in a Living Will.

As stated previously, it is incorrect to associate the elderly with disease and death. Similarly, many elderly are wrongfully stereotyped as unintelligent, unproductive, confused and necessarily burdensome. Hopefully, as this group of citizens grows in numbers, these stereotypes will be forced from the marketplace of ideas by the power inherent in their increased numbers and concentration of wealth.

Although it is claimed that some elderly spend a great deal of time complaining about their maladies, we must consider how often these responses are suggested by questioning their well-being. Which is more redundant, the comments of an elderly person regarding his or her health, or the mindless prodding by one who does not take the time or energy to suggest or introduce other areas of discussion? How many such comments by the elderly are nothing more than the fulfillment of a more youthful inquisitor's expectations? Many elderly are positive and optimistic regarding their well-being and will remain so given the opportunity.

Children play an important role in the lives of their aging parents. Older people frequently rely on the family for their social support. Adult children are frequently the most important source of social contact for the elderly. Most persons over the age of 65 live near but not in the same homes as their children. The elderly's need for privacy and a desire for autonomy encourage them to live in such a fashion. 34

As in all circumstances, planning for the future can greatly reduce the level of anxiety associated with possible shortfalls. For example, concerns over finances may be alleviated by planning for retirement. So too with fears for uncontrolled and undesired future medical treatment. These may be best controlled through a Living Will.

Dealing With Loss

This problem, planning, and answer scenario is not unique to the elderly. Rather, it is shared by all. The elderly do, however, identify areas of concern that may not be as pronounced in other age groups. One such area is loss. The elderly experience certain losses which they are more likely to encounter because of their advanced years. For example, the loss of a spouse to death, or of social and economic status through retirement.

Coupled with the aforementioned are obstacles and losses of another nature. These include a decline in bodily functions such as sight, hearing, and mobility. Add to this the possibility of memory loss and the death of friends and acquaintances, and one might have cause to be concerned with the sorrow in life known as loss.

The issues of independence and autonomy are associated with such losses. The family plays a significant role in this area also. An obvious conflict exists, however, as the elderly may struggle with a need to be autonomous to some degree through independence from their family, but must remain close enough in an effort not to be institutionalized and thereby suffer a much greater loss of freedom.

> *"Home is extraordinarily significant to many older persons. It is a part of their identity, a place where things are familiar and relatively unchanging, and a place to maintain a sense of autonomy and control."* 35

Such an affinity for home is rooted in a desire for freedom and independence, and a fear of loss of contact with familiar things, loved ones, places, death and change. 36

For the elderly, loss of independence is a major source of dissatisfaction. Maintaining independence becomes a primary goal and source of pride. 37 The message from the elderly to society has been stated to include the desire to make their own decisions, the wish to continue to be involved in life, and to be treated with dignity. 38

When dealing with the elderly, and to the extent possible, we should consider these issues of self-determination, the wish to be treated with dignity and the significance of home and familiar environments. Where appropriate and requested, encourage the incorporation of these factors in the life plan and Living Will. This may require discussion of issues such as choice of healthcare facilities and maintenance of contact with family members.

Long Term Healthcare

Another area of concern for the elderly which is closely related to those of autonomy and independence is of future care-giving and institutional placement. Concerns for future long-term care and institutionalization involve worries about the financial burdens that may result as well as emotional issues, including a fear of isolation.

As stated previously, most patients would prefer remaining at home as opposed to an institutional placement although in reality most deaths occur in nursing homes or in hospitals. [39] Whether these concerns by the elderly are based on fear or reason, it has been stated that medical personnel interact less frequently with dying patients, and that patients are often isolated and frequently treated as objects more so than individuals. [40]

Relocation of an elderly and infirm person to an institutional setting, in and of itself, may result in physical and psychological deterioration and even lead to death. [41] Compared to residents in a community setting, institutionalized elders often exhibit an "institutional syndrome" including low morale, a negative self-image, preoccupation with the past, feelings of personal insignificance, intellectual ineffectiveness, docility, withdrawal, anxiety, and fear of death. [42]

Death and Dying

Another significant concern for the elderly is death and dying. As with other facets of their life, the elderly wish to maintain as much control over their dying as possible and to render it meaningful. [43] Death in the present medical environment may be achieved with relief from much physical suffering. This remains a high priority. [44]

The individual should maintain what might truly be considered a lifestyle and be given the opportunity to exercise control and responsibility as long as possible into the dying process. Significantly, those who care for the dying must support the patient's individual decision-making options, pay attention to their privacy and individuality, and support the elder as a knowledgeable participant. Warm and intimate interpersonal relationships with encouragement and reassurance are also of great assistance. 45

What frequently happens, however, is that the dying process is viewed more in the context of the living who must manage the scenario, while the patient ultimately loses control. 46 If death were appropriately viewed as the consummation of a lifetime of thought and endeavor, as much deference as possible would be given to the dying individual.

Death is not necessarily feared by the elderly and is often contemplated with less fear than other concerns. The elderly's attitudes about death most often reflect acceptance. 47

The elderly wish to be prepared and accept death peacefully. Research has shown numerous statements and studies complete with points of view of the elderly on death and the dying process which range from fear of institutional settings to a "bring it on" attitude. The sentiments range from fear to relief and from avoidance to anticipation. Each is valid to the individual and should be respected and reflected in his or her Living Will.

There appears to be a desire expressed by many to die quickly once the dying process begins, naturally and with minimal suffering. Such statements, ones of a similar nature and likely those dissimilar, should not be taken with great surprise, offense, disappointment, or considered abnormal.

Finally, not only should all these areas of concern be addressed, but we might be better equipped to discuss life, death, the quality of life and the process of dying by better understanding the many disorders which typically manifest themselves among the elderly.

Family histories should be reviewed so as to plan for expected genetically driven contingencies. Conditions such as Alzheimer's Disease, arteriosclerosis, strokes, heart disease, arthritis, diabetes and heart attacks, as well as surgery, drug use and abuse and dementia should be discussed with healthcare experts and with those we wish to have involved in the process of preparing and enforcing our Living Wills.

With the warning that you not become overly concerned with the description of the following medical disorders, a brief discussion of some of the better known and feared disabilities which often afflict the elderly is warranted. It may, more than anything else, assist those of lesser years in understanding and appreciating the concerns that some elderly maintain for their future.

Alzheimer's Disease, a highly publicized and much feared disorder, is a progressive and degenerative disease that attacks the brain, impairs memory, the thinking process and behavior. It affects approximately four million Americans and has been identified as the most common form of dementing illness. [48] In excess of one-hundred thousand persons die each year of Alzheimer's Disease and it thereby ranks fourth, behind heart disease, cancer and stroke, in leading causes of death. The disease, over time, results in the inability to perform even routine tasks, disorients and impairs cognitive functions, and generally renders its victims totally incapable of caring for themselves.

There is no known cure for the disease, nor has its cause been identified with certainty. In reality, the best that may be done is to manage some of the stress associated with the disease through medication and planning.

Alzheimer's Disease usually has a duration of from two to ten years but can last much longer. In the latter stages, twenty-four-hour care is required.

Older persons are most frequently afflicted and the disease is estimated to affect approximately 10% of those over age 65 and 47 % of those over age 85. It is frequently diagnosed in a person who later is found to have been suffering from another ailment altogether. This is because Alzheimer's Disease can be definitively diagnosed only after death through an autopsy of brain tissue and in 30% of such cases the result is a different diagnosis. There is a slightly increased risk that family members of one who has suffered from Alzheimer's Disease will also suffer from it, but most cases are the only ones in a given family.

Symptoms may include and escalate from repeating statements, frequent sleeping, perceptual motor problems, and inability to perform other cognitive functions previously enjoyed. Also cited are bouts of suspiciousness; loss of impulse control, weight, short-term memory; incontinence and the need for assistance with all bodily and daily functions.

Parkinson's Disease is another disability often associated with the elderly. It is a neurological disease which causes certain brain cells to degenerate and die, resulting in a host of problems associated with motor activities and dementia. The disease afflicts approximately one-half million Americans and affects approximately one out of every one hundred people over the age of 60. [49] There is no cure for the illness which in and of itself is not fatal. The cause of the disease remains unresolved and is not contagious or likely inherited.

The disease develops over time, usually beginning with a tremor in the extremities, and is often accompanied by problems such as stiffness and rigidity in the joints. The affliction spreads to other areas, often encompassing the entire body. The face may become somewhat mask-like in appearance and the ability to speak deteriorates. Loss of mobility at a most significant level is a major feature of the disease. Symptomology can be controlled to some extent through medication and rehabilitation. An assortment of physiological problems and mental changes accompanies the disease.

Amyotrophic Lateral Sclerosis, also known as **Lou Gehrig's Disease,** is another progressive and fatal neuromuscular condition that attacks cells and pathways in the nervous system.

Each year, at least five thousand men and women in the United States are newly diagnosed with ALS and it is estimated that approximately thirty thousand people suffer from the disease. [50] It is further estimated that approximately three hundred thousand of those people who are presently alive and apparently well in this country will die from ALS.

ALS results in the brain being unable to control muscle movement. Generally, the extremities are affected first with weakening and paralysis thereafter spreading throughout the body. Eventually, speech, swallowing, chewing and breathing are affected. This may often lead to a patient being permanently placed on a ventilator to survive.

Perhaps that which is most heart-wrenching is that intellect and all of the sensor functions are unaffected and the patient is left to view, but not halt, his or her own deterioration.

The average life expectancy of one with ALS ranges from two to three years. Half of all those afflicted live at least three years or more after diagnoses, 20% live five years or more, and approximately 10% survive more than ten years.

The cause or cure of ALS is unknown. It is not contagious and only approximately 5% to 10% of all those suffering from ALS appear to have some associated genetic or inherited component.

The most widespread malady for the aged is **Osteoarthritis.** This is a rheumatic disease which negatively affects the joints, muscles and connecting tissues of the body. Osteoarthritis is long lasting and has no cure. However, it can be managed. It has been estimated that probably every person over 60 years of age has osteoarthritis to some degree. 51 However, it is only of great concern to a much smaller portion of the aging population. There are many suggested causes including a genetic factor and more controllable influences such as obesity.

Unless one has been injured, most persons under the age of 40 years do not notice the symptoms of osteoarthritis. Pain is often localized to certain joint areas but may radiate elsewhere. Weight-bearing joints including hips, knees and the spine are most often involved, as well as finger and toe joints.

There is no known treatment that can reverse the process of osteoarthritis or even prevent it from progressing. It is suggested that the rate of progress may be kept in check and the symptoms reduced by a faithfully followed treatment program frequently involving weight loss, exercise, and medication. Few people will suffer seriously enough to become disabled but, in those incidents, surgery may be helpful. In many cases, one suffering from osteoarthritis can lead a productive and comfortable life.

What must be taken from the synopses of these illnesses which most frequently prey upon the elderly is not a fear of encountering them, but rather understanding that if in fact we do, the period of affliction may be extended and require life-sustaining treatment. Further, they may be accompanied by circumstances that we wish to reflect upon and address in a Living Will.

So as not to leave you with an inappropriately negative association of the elderly with disease or death, it must be noted that approximately 69% of elderly persons described their own health as excellent, very good or good compared with others their age, 20.1% described their health as fair, and only 9.8% as poor. 52

Only about 6% of the elderly have severe dementia. Only 1% of those age 65 to 74 suffer from it and 25% of those age 85 or greater are so impaired. 53 There are approximately 70 conditions that can cause dementia, many of which, as already noted, are often misdiagnosed as uncontrollable Alzheimer's Disease. Of those conditions, however, many are manageable and even reversible.

Beyond the medical perspective, the elderly often show a modest decline in productivity in those jobs requiring significant physical effort. As to other jobs, older workers have been found to perform as well or better than their younger counterparts. Often-stated advantages in employing older workers include fewer avoidable absences from work, greater longevity with the employer and fewer on-the-job accidents. Although speed and performance of certain jobs may decrease, efficiency increases with fewer errors and superior judgment. 54

To dispel yet another myth, researchers have reported that of the elderly studied, 97% claim to enjoy sex, 75% felt that sex was as good or better now than when they were young; 72% were satisfied with their sexual experiences; 80% thought sex was good for their health and 91% approved of unmarried or widowed older people having sexual relations or living together. 55 It certainly appears that the elderly are preoccupied with interests other than their health.

Hopefully these last few lighthearted myth-breakers will help to set aside unfair stereotypes. It is not the intent or purpose of this book to vindicate the elderly. However, to do so may assist in engendering confidence in the elderly who wish to plan for their future medical treatment.

CHAPTER 6

PREPARING A LIVING WILL

Once you have considered whether a Living Will is appropriate for you, reflected upon the moral and practical implications of your choice, discussed the matter with family, friends, attorney and doctor, you are ready to prepare and execute the document.

Communicate Your Decision

One of the most important but frequently forgotten aspects in the Living Will process is assuring that the community is notified of your decision. Of the Living Wills that are executed, many appear not to be reaching hospitals or physicians' offices. Specifically, your attending or primary physician as well as a named proxy decision-maker should be given notice that you have a Living Will. If you know that you will be receiving treatment or care, the institution so providing should also be notified. All of those noticed should receive a copy of the fully executed document.

You should maintain notice of the Living Will's existence on your person at all times. This can be easily accomplished by carrying an identification type card in your wallet or purse containing the information that a Living Will exists, where it is located, and who has copies.

Of those states that have Living Will statutes, there are some basic similarities and numerous differences as the law is not uniform in each jurisdiction. The statute for each state should be reviewed carefully to assure compliance. A discussion of some of the basic similarities and differences that should be of concern will follow to assist in spotting issues and answering core questions.

Signatures and Witnesses

Typically, a Living Will may be drafted for and executed by a competent adult, that being anyone 18 years of age or older who has the capacity to understand the nature and consequence of health-care decisions.

Upon completion, the document will most often need to be signed and dated by the declarant in the presence of two witnesses. They should also state in writing that the declarant was of sound mind and free of duress and undue influence when signing. An extra measure of safety and sometime requirement is to have your Living Will signed and witnessed before a notary public or attorney. All witnesses should, like the declarant, be competent adults.

It may be inappropriate to choose as witnesses any person with an interest in your estate. In those states which permit a surrogate decision-maker, that person should similarly not be a witness. Employees of healthcare facilities where the declarant may be treated should avoid, and in some instances are prohibited, from witnessing a Living Will. Additionally, if one wishes to reaffirm, revoke or change his or her Living Will, it is best that it be done in writing and executed in the fashion previously stated.

Naming A Proxy

In those states that permit a proxy, the declarant should speak with him or her to acquire consent to be named, make certain the directives are understood, and that the proxy agrees to perform accordingly and implement those decisions.

The healthcare representative should be someone whose judgment may be relied upon in the event that circumstances not addressed in the Living Will may arise. As stated previously, the psychological burden on the healthcare representative may be very weighty. Studies show that the willingness to withdraw life-sustaining treatment decreases from

75% to 46% when the decision is not for one's self, but rather for a relative.56 Consider this burden when naming your proxy.

Common sense suggests that the proxy decision-maker should be one likely to outlive the declarant. The choice of a proxy who lives far away should be closely considered as well, as he or she may be difficult to contact or locate and unable to be present and actively involved when needed.

Anyone employed by or associated with a healthcare institution likely to be utilized by the declarant might not be permitted as a healthcare representative. They may be in some instances, however, if related by blood, marriage or adoption. Also, an attending physician may possibly be named as a healthcare representative even if associated with an institution where the declarant is likely to be a patient. However, under such circumstances, the physician would not likely be permitted to participate in rendering a decision as to the patient's competency. These considerations may vary from state-to-state and it is most important that they be discussed with professionals.

It may be appropriate for the declarant to name a contingent healthcare representative in the event that the primary candidate is unable to serve or is unwilling to do so. Whoever is selected as a healthcare representative is subject to any limitations on his or her authority that the declarant may wish to impose. For example, the declarant may permit the healthcare representative to do nothing further than assist in implementation of specific requests expressly stated in the Living Will. At the other end of the spectrum, a healthcare representative may be given broad powers to make any such decisions he or she may feel appropriate after having been guided by a general statement from the declarant.

Please note that the selection of a healthcare representative is not always permitted. In those instances, a Durable Power of Attorney for Healthcare may possibly be utilized to name an agent who will make healthcare decisions.

Declaring Treatment To Be Withheld

Although one may wish to state that all reasonable methods of sustaining life be employed for as long as reasonably possible, almost all Living Wills include a set of circumstances in which life-sustaining treatment is directed to be withheld or withdrawn. It is good practice to include a statement that the declarant understands that such a decision may hasten death and that this conforms with the declarant's general philosophy.

In addition to those circumstances under which life-sustaining treatment may be withheld or discontinued, the Living Will should specifically state whether the declarant wishes artificially provided nutrition and fluids to be treated as a life-sustaining treatment that may be withheld or withdrawn as any other. It must be noted, however, that a number of states do not permit artificially provided hydration and nutrition to be so considered. This area must be reviewed very carefully. Additionally, it may be wise to include a "Do Not Resuscitate Order" as a specific statement in the Living Will as it is a common method of permitting life to expire.

Generally, life-sustaining treatment may be withdrawn or withheld only under certain circumstances. Many states specifically limit those circumstances to cases where a terminal illness is involved. This has been expanded in some states to include when the patient is in a permanently unconscious or vegetative state. The most liberal statutes include permitting the withholding and withdrawal of life-sustaining treatment when it is experimental and likely to be ineffective in prolonging life, or merely prolongs the dying process. Also, the most liberal statutes permit life-sustaining treatment to be withheld or withdrawn when the patient suffers from a serious irreversible illness which is not terminal, and the risks and burdens of treatment to be withheld or withdrawn outweigh the possible benefits to the patient.

It is likely that, over time, those circumstances where life-sustaining treatment may be withheld or withdrawn will be expanded beyond the terminally ill criteria. Hopefully, there will be a successful movement toward uniform legislation in all states.

Many declarants include a specific directive in their Living Will that they be given treatment or medications to alleviate pain. This is entirely appropriate and may be so stated.

Women should consult their state statute for provisions pertaining to termination of life-sustaining treatment by one who is pregnant. It will likely be discovered that, if pregnant, the patient will remain on life support despite a request to the contrary.

Get Professional Advice

I suggest that any declarant utilize the services of an attorney who is experienced in this field. Considering the importance of the content and consequence of the Living Will, it is shortsighted not to take the time and effort and make the modest investment which is likely for the security of knowing that the job is done correctly. Additionally, your attorney should be responsible for notifying the appropriate parties and have sufficient knowledge of the medical field to answer your basic questions regarding healthcare. In some instances, a referral to a medical professional for further discussion may be appropriate.

A knowledgeable legal professional will be able to test your Directive for consistency and enforceability. Your attorney will ensure that the directives are clear, concise, and unambiguous. Thereby, they are more likely to be understood and followed. In many cases, it is simply poor planning to utilize a mass-produced form or a Living Will taken from a magazine.

In the event that your wishes are broader than your state law permits, and if you are intent upon including reasonable requests which are not statutorily provided for, it may not be inappropriate to include your wishes so that at some point in time if the law is expanded, those provisions would become operative. Also, the limiting language in the statute might be challenged in court and found to be unconstitutional and thereby unenforceable.

In these instances, the Living Will should be written in conformance with the statute and include what is often referred to as a "severability clause." This clause states that, should any portion of the document be found illegal or unenforceable, the remaining portion of the document will remain in effect.

CHAPTER 7

PARTING THOUGHTS

In times of adversity, many wish for relief and better times. Some pray and others just "grin and bear it." Frequently, however, adversity remains unplanned for.

A Living Will permits a little of each of the above. It is a statement of your wishes. It is also a prayer of sorts and is most definitely a plan. Even with a Living Will, it is likely there will be much that one who is ill will have to grin and bear. However, the wishes, prayer and plan make it so much easier.

Executing a Living Will can be and often is the type of act which is put off to a later date. Recent legislation, however, will require that all healthcare institutions address the Living Will issue with their patients. This shall make the moment when the Living Will question will arise almost inevitable. Is it not better to make those decisions with a clear head and in familiar surroundings than under the prospect of emergency medical care, illness or hospital admission?

Your Living Will should be a component of a broader life-planning effort. Related to healthcare concerns, one might consider a Durable Power of Attorney for Healthcare which may permit an agent to make medical related decisions for the principal under certain circumstances. For those who can afford additional insurance, policies for extended healthcare are available. Also, planning for Medicaid eligibility for nursing home care may be very important.

There can be little doubt that having a Living Will is one of the best values in healthcare planning. The dollar costs associated with having a Living Will are quite reasonable even when prepared by an attorney with expertise in the area. Although some states do not require that the Advance Directive be renewed periodically, others do, but the costs therefore should be negligible. The price of not having a Living Will, however, might be incalculable.

Financial planning often accompanies concerns for future healthcare. In fact, healthcare planning was often an adjunct or afterthought of financial planning. Most recently, however, health and financial planning have become a means to assuring a certain quality of life. This is an enlightened approach whereby assets are expended upon life rather than vice versa.

This book is not intended to convince you that a Living Will is necessary. Rather, it should be utilized to educate and enhance the likelihood of making an important life decision in a knowing and intelligent manner.

No writing could ever answer the most important questions concerning your Living Will. Only reflection and self-examination will reveal if and when life-sustaining treatment may be withheld or withdrawn, and only you should make that decision.

CHAPTER 8

LIVING WILL EXAMPLES

The following are examples of Living Wills from a few select states. The list is obviously not all inclusive but rather is intended to represent the various forms a Living Will may take.

Read these examples and contemplate including in your Advance Directive those portions with which you agree and feel comfortable. Do not copy or use them as a form for your own Living Will as they may contain provisions that are not recognized in your state. Further, changes might have occurred in the law for those states which are referenced. The first example is one which has been utilized by my office in the State of New Jersey. It is comprehensive if not long-winded.

Note that the preamble to the Directive contains a philosophical statement regarding those functions the declarant feels are important. This general statement is beneficial as there may arise an unforeseen circumstance not specifically addressed in the Living Will. In that case, although the document may be silent on the issue, the healthcare representative, or anyone else who may have cause to review and interpret your intentions, will possess a clear statement of your priorities and approach to the question of withholding or withdrawing life-sustaining treatment.

Secondly, the introductory statement includes a definition of what is regarded as life-sustaining treatment and also what is necessary to be determined incompetent, thereby making your Living Will operational.

A healthcare representative is thereafter named. This option may not be available in your state, but may possibly be cured by creating a Durable Power of Attorney for Healthcare and limiting the agent's powers to those requests set forth in the Living Will. An example of a Durable Power of Attorney is also included. Remember that a surrogate healthcare decision-maker is not required to make your Living Will enforceable. It is merely an option to be considered.

The next section labeled as "Instructional Directive" states the declarant understands that withholding or withdrawing life-sustaining treatment will likely hasten death. This is important as it is a clear statement that you understand the nature of your requests.

The Instructional Directive then lists separate sets of circumstances when life-sustaining treatment may be withheld or withdrawn.

The circumstances for withholding life-sustaining treatment in this example are much more expansive than that which is permitted in most other states. They should be considered and, if desirable, included in your Living Will with a severability clause as described earlier and only if approved by the professional drafting your Living Will.

Next is a statement that artificially provided nutrition and hydration are to be considered life-sustaining treatments. This is included due to the debate discussed earlier. Again, this is more expansive than may be permitted in your state. It may also be considered, however, and discussed with the professionals assisting you.

An item which is sometimes requested to be included is a statement providing anatomical gifts for reasons such as for transplant or research. Although this does not directly touch upon life-sustaining treatment, it may be included in the Directive.

Some states include in their statutes an example of a form that may be used. One such state is Arizona. The Arizona law requires that the declaration shall be substantially in the form provided, but that it may also include other directions. If any of those other specific directions are invalid, that invalidity does not affect other directions that might be followed.

As you can see, the Arizona form is limited to the withholding or withdrawal of life-sustaining procedures in circumstances where the patient is suffering from a terminal condition.

California law provides that its Directive be in the form included. The California Directive is limited to circumstances where the patient suffers from a terminal condition. Hence, one who suffers in a permanently unconscious state may not be permitted to have life-sustaining treatment withheld or withdrawn via a Living Will. Also, the Directive is limited to a period of time and must be renewed thereafter.

Florida is yet another state which limits the withholding and withdrawal of life-prolonging procedures to those suffering from a terminal condition. The form suggested by the Florida statute is also included. Note that the Florida law states that the declaration shall not be operational during pregnancy of the declarant.

As the reader can see from the previous examples, there can be great differences between forms of Living Wills. Acquaint yourself with the form suggested by statute in your state. Whether a form is suggested or not, seek professional guidance, particularly if your directions are more expansive than that permitted by statute.

LIVING WILL
AN ADVANCE DIRECTIVE FOR HEALTHCARE
AND HEALTHCARE REPRESENTATIVE

As a competent adult, I,_____,
hereby wish to memorialize certain healthcare decisions if there may come a time, due to my physical
or mental state, that there has been a loss of decision making capacity to make healthcare decisions.
In that instance, those healthcare institutions and/
or healthcare professionals and/or healthcare repre-
sentatives, responsible for my healthcare and any
and all decisions pertaining thereto, shall take direction herefrom with regard to my healthcare.

There are certain capacities, faculties and functions that I value highly and without which life
would be meaningless, and accordingly should not
be continued. In the event of their loss, I should not
be subjected to life-sustaining treatment. These capacities, faculties and functions include being capable of cogent thought processes and not existing
exclusively and permanently in a confused or unconscious mental state; to be free from debilitating
pain; to maintain some elemental and basic level of
autonomy and be able to care for myself and control my actions at least to the extent that I remain a
participant in my own life; to maintain at some level
my senses to the extent that I may interact with the
environment about me.

Under the cumulative effect of the loss of the aforementioned capacities, faculties and functions, I would be more willing to accept death than continue living as a result of the use of life-sustaining treatment which I identify as the use of any medical devices, procedures, drugs, surgery or therapy that use mechanical or artificial means to sustain, restore, or support a vital bodily function and thereby increase my life expectancy.

This Advance Directive for Healthcare shall take effect in the event I am unable to make my own healthcare decisions, as determined by a physician who has primary responsibility for my care and confirmed by a physician having specialized training or experience in diagnosing mental and physiological conditions or developmental disabilities of a same or similar nature and any and all other confirming determinations as required by Law.

I direct that this document be made part of my permanent medical records and be adhered to explicitly.

HEALTHCARE REPRESENTATIVE

I hereby designate _____, residing at _____, (   ) as my Healthcare Representative to implement and facilitate any and all healthcare decisions for me as I have designated herein. This includes decisions to accept or refuse any treatment, services or procedure used to diagnose or to treat my physical or mental condition, specifically including any life-sustaining treatment, specifically including the withholding or withdrawal of life-sustaining treatment.

I direct that my Healthcare Representative make decisions on my behalf in strict accordance with my directives as stated in this document. To the extent that my Healthcare Representative makes decisions which are contrary or in disagreement with those directives as set forth herein, all such authority he or she has shall terminate.

In the event that my wishes are not clear, or a situation arises which is not anticipated herein, my Healthcare Representative is authorized to make decisions which are in my best interest and based upon the directives set forth herein and what is otherwise known to be my desires.

In the event that my Healthcare Representative should be unable to serve as same for any reasons including refusal, death or the inability to be located and contacted after a diligent search, then I name as contingent Healthcare Representative: _____residing at _____ _____who shall be entrusted with the same rights and authorities as_____.

Should neither be available, I direct that this document continue to be enforceable.

INSTRUCTIONAL DIRECTIVE

So as to advise those persons responsible for my healthcare under those circumstances as set forth herein, I make the following statement of personal views regarding same:

1.   I wish not to have the dying process futilely extended. There are circumstances in which I would not want my life to be prolonged by further medical treatment, including life-sustaining treatment, and under those circumstances same should be withheld or discontinued. I recognize that this will likely hasten my death. I wish life-sustaining treatment only when it is part of the healing process.

2.   I specifically direct that life-sustaining treatment be withheld or withdrawn in the following circumstances:

When I am permanently unconscious, as determined by my attending physician and confirmed by a second qualified physician. A state of permanent unconsciousness shall be when I have been diagnosed in accordance with then current accepted medical standards and within a reasonable degree of medical certainty that there has been a total and irreversible loss of consciousness and capacity for interaction with my environment. This shall include circumstances where I am said to be in a persistent vegetative state or irreversible coma.

When I am in a terminal condition, meaning the terminal stage of an irreversible fatal illness, disease or condition, as determined by my attending physician and confirmed by a second qualified physician. A terminal condition shall not require a certain prognosis of life expectancy with or without the use of life-sustaining treatment. In order to withhold or withdraw life-sustaining measures under these circumstances of a terminal condition, the treatment withheld or withdrawn must be burdensome insofar as same will not promote the likelihood of a cure of my condition but rather serve merely to prolong the process of dying.

When I am diagnosed by my attending physician and same is confirmed by a second qualified physician as suffering from a serious, debilitating, incurable and irreversible illness, disease or condition even though same may not be terminal. This condition must cause me to experience severe and progressive physical and/or mental deterioration and be imminently leading to or having caused the permanent loss of capacities, faculties and functions which I value highly as hereinbefore set forth. Also, the burdens associated with continued life under these circumstances, with life-sustaining treatment, is greater than the benefits I experience thereby.

Under all such circumstances, I direct that I be given the appropriate care to make me comfortable and to relieve pain.

ARTIFICIALLY PROVIDED FLUIDS AND NUTRITION

I consider artificially provided fluids and nutrition such as by feeding tube or intravenous infusion or any other such manners or methods, to be a life-sustaining treatment the same as any other such life-sustaining treatment such as a respirator or like device. I specifically state that there is no difference for the purposes of this directive between artificially provided fluids and/or nutrition and any and all other types of life-sustaining treatment and whenever the phrase "life- sustaining treatment" is stated herein, same shall include artificially provided fluids and/or nutrition. Hence, I specifically direct that artificially provided fluids and/or nutrition may be withheld or withdrawn under any of the following circumstances:

When such treatment is likely to be ineffective or futile in prolonging life, or is likely to merely prolong an imminent dying process.

When I am permanently unconscious, as previously defined herein.

When I am in a terminal condition as previously defined herein and the likely risks and burdens associated with the least burdensome treatment likely to be effective outweighs the likely benefits from such intervention, and if such imposition of the intervention on an unwilling patient would be inhumane.

CARDIOPULMONARY RESUSCITATION

I consider cardiopulmonary resuscitation to be a life-sustaining treatment the same as any such other life-sustaining treatment such as a respirator or like device. I specifically state that there is no difference for the purposes of this directive between cardiopulmonary resuscitation and all other types of life-sustaining treatment and whenever the phrase "life-sustaining treatment" is stated herein, same shall include cardiopulmonary resuscitation. Hence, I specifically direct that cardiopulmonary resuscitation may be withheld or withdrawn under any of the circumtances aforestated herein.

DETERMINATION OF DEATH

I direct that the criteria for determining my time of death be based upon neurological criteria in that I shall be considered to be dead when there has been an irreversible cessation of all functions of the entire brain, including the brain stem.

I understand that there may be such an irreversible cessation of all functions of the entire brain, including the brain stem yet my circulatory and respiratory functions might be maintained by artificial means.

Under the circumstance where there is an irreversible cessation of all functions of the entire brain, including the brain stem, I direct that any artificial means of maintaining my circulatory or respiratory functions be withheld or withdrawn.

ANATOMICAL GIFTS

I wish to make the following anatomical gift to take effect upon my death:

(State request here)

NOTICES

A copy of this document has been provided to:

(Primary Physician, address, telephone #)
(Healthcare Representative, address and
   telephone #)

SIGNATURES

In the event that any part of this declaration is found to be invalid or unlawful, the rest and remainder which is not so held shall remain in full force and effect.

I understand the purpose and the effect of this document and sign it knowingly, intelligently and voluntarily, after giving the entire matter and the contents hereof careful and thoughtful deliberation.

Signed this ____ day of _____, 19____.

NAME: _____

ADDRESS: _____

TELEPHONE NO. _____

I declare that the person who signed this document did so in my presence, that he or she appears to be of sound mind and free of any duress or undue influence. I am 18 years of age or older, and am not designated by this or any other document as the declarant's

Healthcare Representative or Contingent Health-care Representative.

DATE:_____

NAME:_____

ADDRESS: _____

TELEPHONE NO._____

DATE: _____

NAME: _____

ADDRESS: _____

TELEPHONE NO. _____

SUBSCRIBED, SWORN TO AND ACKNOWLEDGED before me by _____, and subscribed and sworn to before me by_____ and _____the witnesses, this_____day of_____, 19___.

DECLARATION

Declaration made this ____ day of _____, ____. I, _____, being of sound mind, willfully and voluntarily make known my desire that my dying not be artificially prolonged under the circumstances set forth below and declare that:

If at any time I should have an incurable injury, disease or illness certified to be a terminal condition by two physicians who have personally examined me, one of whom is my attending physician, and the physicians have determined that my death will occur unless life-sustaining procedures are used and if the application of life-sustaining procedures would serve only to artificially prolong the dying process, I direct that life-sustaining procedures be withheld or withdrawn and that I be permitted to die naturally with only the administration of medication, food or fluids or the performance of medical procedures deemed necessary to provide me with comfort care.

In the absence of my ability to give directions regarding the use of life-sustaining procedures, it is my intention that this declaration be honored by my family and attending physician as the final expression of my legal right to refuse medical or surgical treatment and accept the consequences from such refusal.

I understand the full import of this declaration and I have emotional and mental capacity to make this declaration.

Signed_____
City, County and State of Residence

_____

The declarant is personally known to me and I believe him to be of sound mind.

Witness _____

Witness _____

DIRECTIVE TO PHYSICIANS

Directive made this___day of_____(month, year).
I_____, being of sound mind, willfully, and
voluntarily make known my desire that my life shall
not be artificially prolonged under the circumstances set forth below, do hereby declare:

1. If at any time I should have an incurable injury,
disease, or illness certified to be a terminal condition by two physicians, and where the application of
life-sustaining procedures would serve only to artificially prolong the moment of my death and where
my physician determines that my death is imminent
whether or not life-sustaining procedures are utilized, I direct that such procedures be withheld or
withdrawn, and that I be permitted to die naturally.

2. In the absence of my ability to give directions regarding the use of such life-sustaining procedures,
it is my intention that this directive shall be honored
by my family and physician(s) as the final expression of my legal right to refuse medical or surgical
treatment and accept the consequences from such
refusal.

3. If I have been diagnosed as pregnant and that diagnosis is known to my physician, this directive shall
have no force or effect during the course of my
pregnancy.

4.   I have been diagnosed and notified at least 14 days ago as having a terminal condition by _____ _____, M.D., whose address is _____ _____, and whose telephone number is _____. I understand that if I have not filled in the physician's name and address, it shall be presumed that I did not have a terminal condition when I made out this directive.

5. This directive shall have no force or effect five years from the date filled in above.

6.   I understand the full import of this directive and I am emotionally and mentally competent to make this directive.

Signed _____

City, County and State of Residence

_____

      The declarant has been personally known to me and I believe him or her to be of sound mind.

Witness _____

Witness _____

DECLARATION

Declaration made this_____day of _____, 19__.
I,_____, willfully and voluntarily make
known my desire that my dying not be artificially
prolonged under the circumstances set forth below,
and I do hereby declare:

If at any time I should have a terminal condition
and if my attending physician has determined that
there can be no recovery from such condition and
that my death is imminent, I direct that life prolonging procedures be withheld or withdrawn when the
application of such procedures would serve only to
prolong artificially the process of dying, and that I
be permitted to die naturally with only the administration of medication or the performance of any
medical procedure deemed necessary to provide me
with comfort care or to alleviate pain.

In the absence of my ability to give directions regarding the use of such life-prolonging procedures,
it is my intention that this declaration be honored
by my family and physician as the final expression
of my legal right to refuse medical or surgical treatment and to accept the consequences for such refusal.

If I have been diagnosed as pregnant and that diagnosis is known to my physician, this declaration

shall have no force or effect during the course of
my pregnancy.

I understand the full import of this declaration, and
I am emotionally and mentally competent to make
this declaration.

_____
(Signed)

The declarant is known to me, and I believe him or
her to be of sound mind.

_____
Witness

_____
Witness

POWER OF ATTORNEY FOR HEALTH CARE

1. Designation of Healthcare Agent.

I,_____, hereby appoint _____
_____residing at _____
_____
Home Telephone: _____
Work Telephone: _____
as my Attorney-in-fact (herein referred to as
Agent) to make health and personal care decisions
for me as authorized in this document.

2. Effective Date and Durability.

By this document, I intend to create a Durable Power of Attorney effective upon and only during any
period of incapacity in which, in the opinion of my
Agent and attending physician, I am unable to
make or communicate a choice regarding a particular healthcare decision. This Power of Attorney
shall become effective upon the disability of the
principal.

3. Agent's Power.

I grant to my Agent full authority to make decisions
for me regarding my healthcare. In exercising this
authority, my Agent shall follow my desires as stated in this document or otherwise known to my
Agent. In making any decision, my Agent shall attempt to discuss the proposed decision with me to

determine my desires if I am able to communicate in any way. If my Agent cannot determine the choice I would want made, then my Agent shall make a choice for me based upon what my Agent believes to be in my best interests. My Agent's authority to interpret my desires is intended to be as broad as possible, except for any limitations I may state below. Accordingly, unless specifically limited by Section 4, below, my Agent is authorized as follows.

A. To consent, refuse, or withdraw consent to any and all types of medical care, treatment, surgical procedures, diagnostic procedures, medication, and the use of mechanical or other procedures that affect my bodily functions, including, but not limited to, artificial respiration, nutritional support and hydration, and cardiopulmonary resuscitation;

B. To have access to medical records and information to the same extent that I am entitled to, including the right to disclose the contents to others;

C. To authorize my admission to or discharge even against medical advice from any hospital, nursing home, residential care, assisted living or similar facility or service;

D. To contract on my behalf for any health-care related service or facility on my behalf, without my Agent incurring personal financial liability for such contracts;

E. To hire and fire medical, social service or other support personnel responsible for my care;

F. To authorize, or refuse to authorize, any medication or procedure intended to relieve pain, even though such use may lead to physical damage, addiction, or hasten the moment of, but not intentionally cause, my death;

G. To make anatomical gifts of part or all of my body for medical purposes, authorize an autopsy, and direct the disposition of my remains, to the extent permitted by law;

H. To take any other action necessary to do what I authorize here, including, but not limited to, granting any waiver or release from liability required by any hospital, physician, or other healthcare provider, signing any documents relating to refusals of treatment or the leaving of a facility against medical advice, and pursuing any legal action in my name, and at the expense of my estate to force compliance with my wishes as determined by my Agent, or to seek actual or punitive damages for the failure to comply.

4. **Statement of desires, special provisions, and limitations.**

A. With respect to any life-sustaining treatment, I direct that my Agent follow my Advance Directive for Healthcare or Living Will executed by me.

5. **Nomination of Guardian.**
If a guardian of my person should for any reason be appointed, I nominate my Agent or his or her successor named above.

6. **Administrative Provisions.**

A. I revoke any prior Power of Attorney for healthcare.

B. This Power of Attorney is intended to be valid in any jurisdiction in which it is presented.

C. My Agent shall not be entitled to compensation for services performed under this Power of Attorney, but rather he or she shall be entitled to reimbursement for all reasonable expenses incurred as a result of carrying out any provision of this Power of Attorney.

D. The powers delegated under this Power of Attorney are severable, so that the invalidity of one or more powers shall not affect any others.

BY SIGNING HERE I INDICATE THAT I UNDERSTAND THE CONTENTS OF THIS DOCUMENT AND THE EFFECT OF THIS GRANT OF POWERS TO MY AGENT.

I sign my name to this Healthcare Power of Attorney on this_____day of _____, 19___.

My current home address is _____

_____

Signature: _____
Name: _____

WITNESS STATEMENT.   I declare that the person who signed or acknowledged this document is personally known to me, that he/she signed or acknowledged this Durable Power of Attorney in my presence, and that he/she appears to be of sound mind and under no duress, fraud, or undue influence. I am not the person appointed as Agent by this document, nor am I the patient's healthcare provider or an employee of the patient's healthcare provider. I further declare that I am not related to the Principal by blood, marriage or adoption, and, to the best of my knowledge, I am not a creditor of the Principal nor entitled to any part of his/her estate under a Will now existing or by operation of Law.

WITNESS NO. 1

Signature:_____
Date: _____
Print Name:_____
Telephone: _____
Residence Address: _____

WITNESS NO. 2

Signature: _____
Date: _____
Print Name: _____
Telephone: _____
Residence Address: _____

NOTARIZATION, STATE OF _____,
COUNTY OF _____.
On this____day of _____,19___ , the said _____
_____, known to me or satisfactorily prov-
en to be the person named in the foregoing instrument, personally appeared before me, a Notary Public, within and for the State and County aforesaid,
and acknowledged that he or she freely and voluntarily executed the same for the purposes stated
therein.

My Commission Expires:

_____   _____
                          Notary Public

ENDNOTES

Preface

1. Carol J. Dufraine, "*Living Wills--A Need For Statewide Legislation or a Federally Recognized Right?*" 1983 Detroit College of Law Review, page 781.

Why A Living Will

2. Ted Gest with Steven Findlay, Dorian R. Friedman and Richard Z. Chesnoff, "*Changing The Rules On Dying,*" U.S. News and World Report, July 9, 1990, page 22.

3. John Edward Ruark, M.D., Thomas Alfred Raffin, M.D., and The Stanford University Medical Center Committee On Ethics, "*Initiating And Withdrawing Life Support; Principles And Practice In Adult Medicine,*" New England Journal Of Medicine, Number 1, Volume 318, January 7, 1988, page 26.

Case Studies in the Withholding and Withdrawal of Life-sustaining Treatment

4. In re Conroy, 98 N.J. 321, 486 A.2d 1209, 1220 (1985).

5. Id. at 1229.

6. Id. at 1244.

7. In re Farrell, 108 N.J. 335, 529 A.2nd 404, 409 (1987).

8. Saunders v. State, 492 N.Y.S. 2nd 510, 517 (Sup. Ct. 1985).

9. Id. at 517.

Things To Consider

10. John Edward Ruark, M.D., Thomas Alfred Raffin, M.D., and The Stanford University Medical Center Committee On Ethics, *"Initiating and Withdrawing Life Support; Principles And Practice In Adult Medicine,"* New England Journal Of Medicine, Number 1, Volume 318, January 7, 1988, page 27.

11. Ibid, page 29, 30.

12. Jerry Buckley, *"How Doctors Decide Who Shall Live And Who Shall Die,"* U.S. News And World Report, January 22, 1990, page 57.

13. Judith Waldrop and Thomas Exter, *"What The 1990 Census Will Show,"* American Demographics, January 1990, page 27.

14. James R. Wetzel, *"American Families: 75 Years of Change,"* Monthly Labor Review, March 1990, page 5.

15. Ibid., page 10.

16. U.S. Senate Special Committee on Aging in Conjunction with the American Association of Retired Persons, The Federal Council on the Aging, and the U.S. Administration on Aging, Aging America Trends And Projections, 1987-1988 edition, page 97.

17. James R. Wetzel, *"American Families: 75 Years of Change,"* Monthly Labor Review, March 1990, page 5.

18. Ibid., page 10.

19. Ibid.

20. Judith Rodin and Jeanette R. Ickovics, *"Women's Health, Review and Research Agenda As We Approach The 21st Century,"* American Psychologist, Volume 45, Number 9, September 1990, page 1018.

21. New Jersey Department Of Community Affairs Division On Aging, Aging In New Jersey Sixty-Five And Over, August 1985, page 46.

22. Judith Rodin and Jeanette R. Ickovics, *"Women's Health, Review and Research Agenda as We Approach the 21st Century,"* American Psychologist, Volume 45, Number 9, September 1990, page 1018.

23. Ibid., page 1029.

24. U.S. Senate Special Committee On Aging In Conjunction With The American Association Of Retired Persons, The Federal Council On The Aging, and the U.S. Administration on Aging, Aging America Trends And Projections, 1987-1988 edition, page 102.

25. Peter Kemper and Christopher M. Murtaugh, *"Lifetime Use Of Nursing Home Care,"* New England Journal Of Medicine, Volume 324, Number 9, February 28, 1991, page 595.

26. Ibid.

27. Ibid.

28. Ibid., page 597.

29. Ibid.

30. Sidney H. Wanzer, M.D., et al., *"The Physician's Responsibility Towards Hopelessly Ill Patients; A Second Look,"* New England Journal Of Medicine, Volume 320, Number 13, March 30, 1989, page 846.

31. Nancy Gibbs, *"Love And Let Die,"* Time Magazine, March 19, 1990, page 65.

Thinking Elderly

32. Nancy R. Hooyman and H. Asuman Kiyak, Social Gerontology: A MultiDisciplinary Perspective, 2nd edition, Allyn and Bacon (A Division Of Simon and Schuster,Inc.), Needham Heights, Massachusetts, 1988, page 255.

33. Ibid., page 431.

34. Ibid., page 306.

35. Robert N. Butler and Myrna I. Lewis, <u>Aging And Mental Health Positive Psychosocial And Biomedical Approaches</u>, 3rd edition, C.V. Mosby Company, St. Louis, Missouri, 1982, page 255.

36. Ibid.

37. William H. Quinn and George A. Hughston, <u>Independent Aging: Family and Social Systems Perspectives,</u> Aspen Systems Corporation, Rockville, Maryland, Royal Tunbridge Wells, 1984, page 257.

38. Robert N. Butler and Myrna I. Lewis, <u>Aging and Mental Health Positive Psychosocial and Biomedical Approaches</u>, 3rd edition, C.V. Mosby Company, St. Louis, Missouri, 1982, page vii.

39. Nancy R. Hooyman and H. Asuman Kiyak, <u>Social Gerontology: A MultiDisciplinary Perspective</u>, 2nd edition, Allyn and Bacon, (A Division Of Simon and Schuster, Inc.), Needham Heights, Massachusetts, 1988, page 431.

40. Ibid.

41. Russel A. Ward, <u>The Aging Experience: An Introduction To Social Gerontology,</u> 2nd edition, Harper and Row Publishers, Inc., New York, 1984, page 293.

42. Ibid.

43. Ibid., page 340.

44. Ibid., page 341.

45. Ibid.

46. Ibid., pages 332, 333 and 342.

47. Ibid., page 326.

48. Alzheimer's Disease related information taken from National Academy of Elder Law Attorneys, 3rd Annual Symposium on Elder Law, Promoting Independence: Helping To Keep The Client At Home, May 15-18, 1991, Orlando, FL., citing *Someone To Stand By You,* Alzheimer's Disease and Related Disorders Assoc. Inc., Chicago, IL.

49. Parkinson's Disease related information taken from National Academy of Elder Law Attorneys, 3rd Annual Symposium on Elder Law, Promoting Independence: Helping To Keep The Client At Home, May 15-18, 1991, Orlando, FL.

50. Amyotrophic Lateral Sclerosis related information taken from National Academy of Elder Law Attorneys, 3rd Annual Symposium on Elder Law, Promoting Independence: Helping To Keep The Client At Home, May 15-18, 1991, Orlando, FL.

51. Osteoarthritis related information taken from National Academy of Elder Law Attorneys, 3rd Annual Symposium on Elder Law, Promoting Independence: Helping To Keep The Client At Home, May 15-18, 1991, Orlando, FL.

52. National Academy of Elder Law Attorneys, 3rd Annual Symposium on Elder Law, Introduction to Elder Law, May 15, 1991, Orlando, FL., citing the 1987 *National Health Interview Survey.*

53. Ibid., citing the 1987 Federal Office of Technology Assessment Report.

54. Ibid., citing the Journal of Gerontology, and the Journal of Industrial Gerontology.

55. Ibid., citing the Starr-Weiner Report (1981).

Preparing A Living Will

56. Linda L. Emanuel and Ezekiel J. Emanuel, *"The Medical Directive: A New Comprehensive Advance Care Document,"* Journal Of The American Medical Association, Volume 261, Number 22, June 9, 1989, page 3289.

BIBLIOGRAPHY

American Association of Retired Persons, <u>Tomorrow's Choices:
Preparing Now For Future Legal, Financial and Health Care
Decisions</u>. Washington, D.C., 1988.

<u>Bartling v. Super Ct.</u> 209 Cal. Rpt. 220 (Dist. Ct. App. 1984).

Besson Paul B., M.D., Walsh McDermott, M.D., and James B.
Wyngaarden, M.D., <u>Cecil Textbook of Medicine</u>, 15th edition,
Volume 1, W.B. Saunders Company, Philadelphia, Pennsylvania,
East Sussex, England and Toronto, Ontario, Canada, 1979.

Buckley, Jerry, "*How Doctors Decide Who Shall Live And Who Shall
Die,*" <u>U.S. News And World Report</u>, January 22, 1990.

Butler, Robert N. And Myrna I. Lewis, <u>Aging And Mental Health
Positive Psychosocial And Biomedical Approaches</u>, 3rd edition,
C.V. Mosby Company, St. Louis, Missouri, 1982.

Condie, Christopher J., "*Comparison Of The Living Will Statutes Of
The Fifty States,*" 14, <u>Journal Of Contemporary Law</u>, 1988.

<u>Cruzan v. Director, Missouri Department of Health,</u> 110 Sup. Ct. 2841
(1990).

Dufraine, Carol J., "*Living Wills - A Need For Statewide Legislation Or
A Federally Recognized Right?*" <u>1983 Detroit College Of Law
Review</u>.

Emanuel, Linda L., And Ezekiel J. Emanuel, "*The Medical Directive, A
New Comprehensive Advance Care Document,*" <u>Journal Of The
American Medical Association</u>, Volume 261, Number 22, June 9,
1989, Page 3288.

Episcopal Church, resolution: <u>Living Will</u> (C-008), approved at the 70th
General Convention, Phoenix, Arizona, 1991.

Francis, Leslie Pickering, "*The Evanescence Of Living Wills,*" 24, <u>Real
Property, Probate and Trust Journal,</u> Spring, 1989.

General Commission On Christian Unity And Interreligious Concerns Of The United Methodist Church And The Bishops' Committee For Ecumenical And Interfaith Affairs, National Conference Of Catholic Bishops, Holy Living And Holy Dying, A United Methodist And Roman Catholic Common Statement, 1989.

Gest, Ted, Steven Findlay, Dorian R. Friedman, and Richard Z. Chesnoff, "Changing The Rules On Dying," U.S. News And World Report, July 9, 1990.

Gibbs, Nancy, "Love And Let Die," Time Magazine, March 19, 1990.

Hooyman, Nancy R., And H. Asuman Kiyak, Social Gerontology: A MultiDisciplinary Perspective, 2nd edition. Allyn and Bacon, A Division Of Simon and Schuster, Needham Heights, Massachusetts, Inc., 1988.

In re Conroy, 98 N.J. 321, 486 A.2d 1209 (1985).

In re Farrell, 108 N.J. 335, 529 A.2d 409 (1987).

In re Jobes, 108 N.J. 394, 529 A.2d 434 (1987).

In re N, 406 A.2d 1275 (1979, Dist. Col. App.).

In re Quinlan, 70 N.J. 10, 355 A.2d 647 (1976).

In re Visbeck, 210 N.J. Super. 527 (Chan. Div. 1986), 510 A.2d 125 (1986).

Kemper, Peter, PH.D., and Christopher M. Murtaugh, PH.D., "Use Of Nursing Home Care," New England Journal Of Medicine, Volume 324, Number 9, February 28, 1991.

Malfa, Matthew, "Legislative Deliberations, Life and Death Issues: New Jersey Debates Living Wills and The Declarations of Death," 13, Seton Hall Legislative Journal, 1990.

National Academy of Elder Law Attorneys, 3rd Annual Symposium on Elder Law, Introduction to Elder Law, May 15-18, 1991, Orlando, FL.

National Academy of Elder Law Attorneys, 3rd Annual Symposium on Elder Law, Promoting Independence: Helping To Keep The Client At Home, May 15-18, 1991, Orlando, FL.

New Jersey Department Of Community Affairs Division on Aging, Ann Zahora, Director, Aging In New Jersey Sixty-Five And Over, State Of New Jersey Department Of Community Affairs, John P. Renna, Commissioner, Division On Aging, August 1985.

Quinn, William H. and George A. Hughston, Independent Aging: Familyand Social Systems Perspectives, Aspen Systems Corporation, Rockville, Maryland, Royal Tunbridge Wells, 1984.

Rabbinical Assembly, Rabbi Elliot N. Dorff, A Jewish Approach To End-Stage Medical Care, December 1990 and Rabbi Avram Israel Reisner, A Halakhic Ethic Of Care For The Terminally Ill, 1990.

Rodin, Judith And Jeanette R. Ickovics, *"Women's Health, Review And Research Agenda As We Approach The 21st Century,"* American Psychologist, Volume 45, Number 9, September 1990.

Rosoff, Sidney D., *"Where There's A Living Will, There's A Way,"* The Compleat Lawyer, Fall, 1988.

Ruark, John Edward, M.D., Thomas Alfred Raffin, M.D., and The Stanford University Medical Center Committee On Ethics, *"Initiating And Withdrawing Life Support Principles And Practice In Adult Medicine,"* New England Journal of Medicine, Volume 318, Number 1, January 7, 1988.

Sabatino, Charles P., American Bar Associates Commission On Legal Problems Of The Elderly, Health Care Powers Of Attorney, Distributed in Cooperation with the American Association of Retired Persons, American Bar Association, 1990.

Saunders v. State, 492 N.Y.S. 2d 510 (Sup. Ct. 1985).

State of New Jersey Commission on Legal and Ethical Problems in the Delivery of Health Care (The New Jersey Bioethics Commission), <u>Advance Directives for Health Care</u>, and related materials contained within, March, 1991.

United Methodist Church, <u>The Book Of Discipline of The United Methodist Church</u>, The United Methodist Publishing House, Nashville, Tennessee, 1988.

U.S. Senate Special Committee On Aging In Conjunction With The American Association Of Retired Persons, The Federal Council On The Aging, And The U.S. Administration On Aging, <u>Aging America Trends And Projections</u>, 1987-1988 edition.

Waldrop, Judith and Thomas Exter, *"What The 1990 Census Will Show,"* <u>American Demographics</u>, January 1990, Page 27.

Wanzer, Sidney H., M.D., Daniel D. Federman, M.D.,S., James Adelstein, M.D., Christine K. Cassel, M.D., Edwin H. Cassem, M.D., Ronald E. Cranford, M.D., Edward W. Hook, M.D., Bernard Lo, M.D., Charles G. Moertel, M.D., Peter Safar, M.D., Allan Stone, M.D., and Jan van Eys, Ph.D., M.D., *"The Physician's Responsibility Towards Hopelessly Ill Patients; A Second Look,"* <u>New England Journal Of Medicine</u>, March 30, 1989.

Ward, Russell A., <u>The Aging Experience: An Introduction To Social Gerontology</u>, 2nd edition. New York, Harper And Row Publishers, Inc., New York, 1984.

Wetzel, James R., *"American Families: 75 Years Of Change,"* <u>Monthly Labor Review</u>, March 1990. (1987).

INDEX

The author welcomes inquiries and comments about *To Live And Die With Dignity, A Guide To Living Wills.* He is also available for speaking engagements for your group or organization. Please write or fax:

SAMUEL L. PELUSO, ESQ.
473 Broadway
Long Branch, NJ 07740
Office Telephone: (908) 222-3338
Fax: (908) 222-7421